GRANDMOTHER'S WISDOM

GRANDMOTHER'S WISDOM

Good old-fashioned advice
handed down through the ages

LEE FABER

Michael O'Mara Books Limited

This paperback edition first published in 2017

First published in Great Britain in 2009 by
Michael O'Mara Books Limited
9 Lion Yard
Tremadoc Road
London SW4 7NQ

ISBN: 978-1-78243-824-3 in paperback
ISBN: 978-1-84317-841-5 in EPub format
ISBN: 978-1-84317-840-8 in Mobipocket format

1 2 3 4 5 6 7 8 9 10

www.mombooks.com

Illustrations copyright © David Woodroffe 2009
Designed and typeset by Omigie Design
Printed and bound by CPI Group (UK) Ltd, Croydon, CR0 4YY

Contents

Remedies

Food and Cooking: The Basics

Recipes

Plants and Pets

Advice about Children

Families and Daily Life

Acknowledgements

A lot of people helped me in the writing of this book – my children and grandchildren, my parents, my sister, other members of my family and friends whose experiences are cited here; Louise Dixon at Michael O'Mara for commissioning me in the first place; my editor, Hannah Knowles, who encouraged me all along; and my wonderful husband, John, who has had to listen to and read *ad infinitum* everything I decided to include.

To Kelly, Chris, Austen, Sophie
and Jared, my grandchildren, without whom
I could never have written this book.

Introduction

What would we do without our grannies?

The current crop of grandmothers are very different creatures from most grandmothers in previous centuries. We juggle jobs, households, families and grandchildren and somehow even find time for our friends, fun and a bit of pampering.

We generally look different, too – younger and fitter. We also have new ways of doing things because we have new labour-saving devices, but that doesn't mean we have turned our backs on traditional, old-fashioned methods and ingredients. Why? Because they still work.

From time immemorial, we, as little children, have perched on kitchen steps and countertops by granny's side or followed her like small shadows as she set about her work.

And through osmosis, we absorbed and learned. And when we grew up and got older, the little children started to watch us. And so it goes on: the lore is not lost.

Grandma knows best

This email came to me from an American friend and, for me, defines what grandmother's wisdom is all about!

My four-year-old granddaughter picked something off the ground while we were out, and raised it to her mouth. I took the item from her and told her not to do that.

'Why?' she asked.

'Because it's been on the ground. It's dirty, and probably has germs,' I replied.

My granddaughter looked at me admiringly and asked, 'How do you know all this stuff? You're so smart.' I was thinking quickly.

'All Grandmas know this stuff. It's on the Grandma Test. You have to know it, or you can't be a Grandma.'

We walked in silence for a couple of minutes, but she was evidently pondering this new information.

'Oh... I get it!' she beamed, 'So if you don't pass the test, you have to be the Grandpa.'

'Exactly,' I replied, with a big smile.

Throughout this book I've tried to gather together all those timeless gems of advice that grandmothers have passed down through the generations – and have added a sprinkle of my own personal experience, too. Hopefully you will find it so useful that you continue the tradition, and keep spreading the wisdom.

Household Hints

The kitchen

Our own grandmothers had a pretty good idea how to keep their kitchens clean, but they weren't as obsessed with kitchen hygiene as we have become.

Keeping everything as clean as possible in the area in which we prepare food is a given, but there is no need to keep lots of bottles of chemicals under the sink to do so. Most things can be cleaned perfectly well with six old-fashioned ingredients: vinegar, salt, soda water, lemon, cream of tartar and bicarbonate of soda. Just like our grandmothers did.

They certainly didn't have colour-coded cutting boards. Nor do I. I have a twenty-five-year-old wooden board, which I keep scrupulously clean with a table knife, steel wool and bicarbonate of soda. Sometimes if I have a tomato or berry stain on the board, I cheat a little by rubbing the stain with a cut lemon.

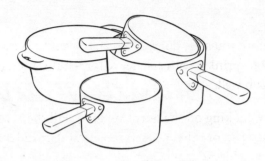

Pots and pans

Removing burnt food from cookware can be a nightmare. As long as the pan isn't non-stick, the scouring powder and alternative methods below will work beautifully, and because they use natural ingredients, you won't have to worry about residual chemicals.

Make your own scouring powder

You can make your own gentle cleaner with no artificial ingredients or harmful chemicals that will work as well on porcelain sinks and easily scratchable countertops. Just add one cupful of salt to one cupful of bicarbonate of soda and blend well. Store in a covered container and keep with your other cleaning supplies.

When you need to use it, shake a little of the mixture on to a wet cloth and scour as usual. You'll find your pots and pans come up sparkling clean. Below are some alternative techniques, most involving the extremely handy bicarbonate of soda.

- Before you start doing the dishes, wet the burnt spot, sprinkle with salt, leave for ten minutes, then scrub well.

- Try cooking off the burnt-on food. Fill the saucepan or other cookware with water, add 30ml (two tablespoons) bicarbonate of soda and reheat on the hob. Bring the water to the simmer over a medium heat and use a spatula to scrape the food from the pan. Turn off the heat and let the pan sit on the hob until the water has cooled. At that point you can wash the food away without any fuss or additional elbow grease.

- Leave the pan to soak in a bicarbonate of soda solution for ten minutes before washing. Alternatively, scrub the pan with dry bicarb and a moist scouring pad.

- For badly burnt pans, sprinkle a thick layer of bicarbonate of soda on to the bottom of the pan, and then sprinkle with just enough water to moisten. Leave to soak overnight, then scrub clean.

- For non-stick pans, make a paste of bicarbonate of soda and water. Transfer to a cloth and scrub the pan gently. This will lift the grease, but won't harm the coating of the pan. It will also get rid of persistent cooking odours.

✷ The bicarb trick also works on roasting tins and microwave turntables. First sprinkle the tin or turntable with the soda and leave for a moment, then mix four parts water with one part white vinegar and pour into the tin or sprinkle over the turntable. It will fizz up and lift the grease.

✷ If your pans are aluminium and you need to remove stains, mix some cream of tartar, which is a mild acid, with enough boiling water to make a paste, then apply.

Coffee or tea stains on cups

You don't have to resort to bleach to remove stains from light-coloured cups and mugs. A much healthier alternative is salt. Simply scrub the stains with a sponge or cloth sprinkled with salt or – if you need a heavier-duty cleaner – mix up a solution of equal parts salt and distilled malt vinegar.

Cleaning the kitchen sink

Whether your kitchen sink is stainless steel, porcelain, cast iron or acrylic, to keep it at its pristine cleanest you should wash it or at least rinse and buff it with a soft cloth every time you use it.

Even if you don't throw grease down the drain, the very nature of the kitchen sink ensures that the drain will get clogged because you are constantly washing greasy dishes and pans, and eventually it could begin to smell disgusting. To keep your drain clean and free-flowing, mix enough salt in a jug of warm water to make the water cloudy, pour it down the drain. Give it about fifteen minutes, then run fresh water into it.

The actual sink can be cleaned with a sprinkling of bicarbonate of soda and a spritz of white vinegar from a spray bottle. Or you can sprinkle with bicarb, cut a lemon in half and use the cut end as your scourer. It will smell lovely, too.

If you have a ceramic sink stained by tea, a good trick is to sprinkle it with dishwashing powder, leave it for thirty minutes or so, then scrub with a non-metallic pad or micro-fibre cloth.

Fizzy soda water is an effective cleaner for stainless steel sinks and cutlery.

Antibacterial soap

This is one product my grandmother never had sitting on her kitchen counter – and something I would never be without. This I learned the hard way.

One Christmas I gave myself blood poisoning as the result

of stuffing a free-range turkey (which was rife with bacteria) when I had a cut on my thumb. By Boxing Day, the red line was starting to travel up my arm and it was off to the A & E pretty fast. A tetanus shot and a low sling did the job, but a chef friend taught me always to have antibacterial soap on the sink and to use it after preparing any raw food. I have never regretted this advice.

Cleaning chrome

I have a nice chrome toaster sitting on my kitchen counter. I also have chrome taps in my kitchen and bathrooms. While you can wash the taps with soapy water, you should never immerse a toaster. If you are going to use soap for the toaster, unplug it first, then wipe it with a soapy cloth or sponge and wipe with a non-soapy cloth. To remove fingerprints and to make the chrome really shine, spray with window cleaner or buff with a bit of silver polish.

Ovenproof glass or porcelain dishes

To loosen baked-on food from ovenproof glass or porcelain casserole dishes, boil 60ml (2fl oz) white vinegar with 450ml (15fl oz) water and leave the dishes to soak in the solution overnight. (You may need to mix up a bigger quantity if the dishes are large.) Wash the dishes afterwards in some hot, soapy water.

Cleaning the oven

Everyone's least favourite job is cleaning the oven. However, this little trick will save a lot of elbow grease later. Before you start to wash the dishes after your evening meal, mix together a solution of 180ml (6fl oz) boiling water and 60ml (2fl oz) white vinegar and use it to wipe the walls and floor of the oven while it is still warm (*not* hot, warm) – you will find that you won't need to apply an industrial-strength cleaner later.

Keeping smells out of your refrigerator and freezer

My mother always kept an open box of bicarbonate of soda in the refrigerator because it neutralizes odours, and I do the same (although mine is in a little Styrofoam snowman). You can also use it in the freezer. Remember to change the box every three months to keep it fresh. To help you remember, write the date you first started using it on the box.

Sticky stuff

When working with sticky stuff in the kitchen, there are two solutions – latex gloves and vegetable oil spray.

- When measuring honey, golden syrup and treacle, spray or smear a little vegetable oil on the spoon or cup you will be using to measure. The sticky substance will just slide off.

- When working with sticky dough, breadcrumb coatings, meatloaf mixes or chocolate, first make sure you have everything to hand that you need. Wearing gloves can help, as you can knead, squelch and mix to your heart's delight, then just slip the gloves off into the rubbish bin if the mixture was really sticky, or wash your hands with the gloves on, then dry and slip them off for use another time.

- When using superglue, first prepare the surface you will be working on. Parchment paper does it for me. Newspaper and kitchen paper tend to stick to the object you are gluing. Then put on the gloves and open the glue. Holding the broken pieces over the parchment, spread glue on the surfaces that you will be sticking together. Then press them together and hold for the count of a hundred. Place the repaired item on the parchment and allow to dry completely. It should be stuck together securely and not stuck to the parchment!

Clean your bathroom in twenty minutes

Having more than just one 'family bathroom' in your house has its pros and cons. On the plus side, you don't have to wait forever to use the facilities when someone is just dawdling in there, but on the minus side, think about all that extra cleaning!

With a good routine you can have it both ways. If your bathrooms have been neglected, it might take a little longer the first time, but after that, it will be a breeze. Once a week for a 'clean' should be sufficient unless your bathroom has a lot of traffic.

1. Remove ornaments from shelves and windowsills and put them in the hall. Remove and replace the towels and bath mat if necessary, putting the used ones in the laundry.

2. Sweep or vacuum the floor.

3. Spray the sink and countertops with the cleaner of your choice and leave it to work while you do your next tasks.

4. Clean the mirror.

5. Spray the bath with cleaning spray, and turn on the shower to rinse, or if you have a shower enclosure, spray the walls, then

rinse with the shower. If you spray the shower enclosure door every day after your shower, it will be easy to keep clean. In the same way, if you are a bath person, clean the bath after you have bathed and you won't have any 'rings' to clean later.

6.   Spray the inside of the toilet and leave the cleaner to work.

7.   Scrub your sink and countertops, then rinse and wipe dry with a clean cloth. Use the cloth to give your taps a nice polish.

8.   Scrub the inside of your toilet with a toilet brush. Flush to rinse. Wipe the outside of the toilet with a cloth that has been dipped in disinfectant or borax and wrung out. Don't forget the areas behind the seat, outside the bowl and the base.

9.   Mop the floor if it is washable. If the bathroom is tiny, like mine, you can spray the cleaner on the floor and wipe it with a sponge or cleaning cloth. Let dry for ten to fifteen minutes.

That's pretty much it. If you have ornaments, you will have to dust or wash them as is appropriate.

Limescale

Limescale is a very common problem, and can spoil your morning cup of tea or coffee if you don't tackle it quickly. Here are some tried and tested – and natural – tips for getting rid of it.

Taps and showerheads

If you have the sort of mixer tap you can unscrew, soak it overnight in white vinegar. If not, poke a wooden toothpick into the holes. This should free it of gunk. This works for showerheads too.

Kettles

Kettles need to be descaled, not only because you end up with flakes in your tea, but also because a furry kettle takes longer to heat up and will probably die sooner. You can use either vinegar or lemon.

If you choose vinegar use one part white vinegar to one part water. Pour into the kettle and allow to soak. If the vinegar smell does not disappear right away, you could squeeze the juice of one lemon into 300ml (10fl oz) water. Boil it up in the kettle, then empty and rinse – it will smell lovely.

The toilet

Unsightly marks under the rim of the toilet that just can't be removed by any other means can be taken care of easily with a pumice stone. Just rub the pumice over the marks, then brush as usual.

Two denture tablets thrown into the toilet bowl will also clean the parts your brush can't reach.

Vinegar, the miracle cleaner

If you look under your kitchen sink, you will probably find a dozen or so cleaners that have specific purposes – window cleaners, floor cleaners, oven cleaners, deodorizers and then some.

You can throw them all in the bin and replace with one inexpensive miracle cleaner that will not only make everything in your kitchen spotless and sparkling, but is useful for every room in your house. You might have a bottle of it in your kitchen, as did your mother, your grandmother and your great grandmother. It's called white vinegar.

This mild acid will clean and shine nearly everything in your home. Mix one part vinegar to five parts water to clean windows and spectacles. Use it full strength to kill stale food odours in food containers. Soak your showerhead in it to remove limescale. Moisten a cloth with vinegar and wipe your oven walls and hob to prevent greasy build-up. Dilute it with water in a saucepan and boil to remove unpleasant cooking odours. And that's just for starters. You will find more specific information throughout this section of the book.

Getting rid of moths

Moths can be an absolute scourge to your household – getting into your food cupboards and eating holes in your clothes. Here is some advice for tackling them:

Moths in the kitchen

✖ When you buy flour, grains and dry foods, store them in the freezer for a couple of days. Then you can safely put the packages in your cupboard. When you open the package, if you don't use all of the contents, store the remainder in clean jam jars, mayonnaise jars or airtight plastic containers.

✖ Keep opened bags of flour enclosed in plastic bags in the refrigerator, and with any luck you won't have any more infestations. Put up tacky strips on the insides of your cupboards to trap the moths.

Moths in your clothes

❀ Make sure you wash or dry clean all your clothes at the first sign of moths, spray your wardrobes with mothkiller and hang mothballs as a repellent.

❀ Dehumidifiers can help deter moths since they keep the air too dry for the insects.

❀ Ironing your clothes should help to kill any larvae present in the fabrics.

❀ If all else fails, you will have to call out the pest control people as a full-scale infestation will be impossible to control without this.

Picking up broken glass

Breaking something made out of glass is such a problem. No matter how many times you sweep or vacuum, there always seem to be little slivers lurking about. The best way to deal with those microscopic shards on a hard floor surface is to dampen a sturdy sheet of kitchen paper and wipe it over the whole area. Do this several times (with new paper) until you no longer see glints of glass. And don't poke the paper or you'll surely cut yourself and then you'll have new problems. However, this doesn't work for carpets, as I found out recently when I *did* cut my finger. There, a dustpan and brush is the best pick-up method.

Recycling torn tights

When your tights have holes and ladders, don't discard them. They still have a lot of life left in them. Here are some useful ways to recycle them:

❊ When you drop something small on the floor (for example an earring, needle, vitamin tablet, etc.) and can't see or feel it, cut the leg off a pair of tights and put it over the nozzle of your vacuum cleaner. The suction will lift the item off the floor and on to the fabric.

❊ After you polish a pair of shoes, rub them with a balled up pair of old tights for an extra shine.

❊ Store onions in an old pair of tights. Just drop them into the legs, hang the tights up and the onions will keep longer. Flower bulbs can be stored in the same way, and will be protected from little creatures looking for food.

❊ When repotting your houseplants, cut a circle of nylon from the tights the same diameter as the bottom of the pot, and put it in before filling with some small stones and then compost. This stops the compost from falling through the bottom of the pot every time you water the plant.

❊ Cut the tights into strips and use to stuff cushions, pillows and soft toys.

Toothbrushes clean more than teeth

Old toothbrushes are fantastically useful for reaching into the small places that other cleaning methods can't reach. Some areas can be cleaned with a dry brush, while others will do better with a wet brush that has been dipped in vinegar or bleach. These are only a few ideas. You will discover many more on your own.

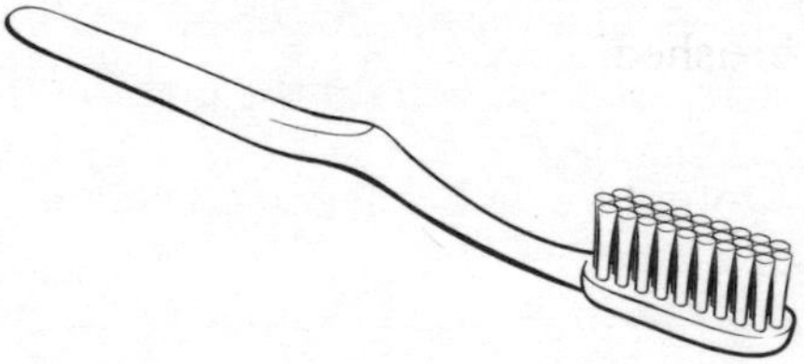

In the bathroom

- Use an old toothbrush to scrub the tracks on sliding shower doors.
- Brush the underside of bathroom taps and the place where the taps join the sink with a vinegar-soaked toothbrush.
- Soak showerheads in vinegar, then scrub with an old toothbrush.
- The grout between tiles can also be sprayed with vinegar. After a few minutes, scrub away at it with the toothbrush.

In the kitchen

- Oven and cupboard doorknobs can be de-gunked with an old toothbrush.

- If you use a manual can opener, a toothbrush is perfect for cleaning the wheels.

- The seal around the kitchen sink that collects coffee grinds and other debris will benefit from being brushed.

- Brush around the hob where it meets the kitchen counter.

The rest of the house

- Crayon marks can be removed with a small amount of toothpaste on a wet toothbrush. Wipe off with a damp cloth or sponge.

- Brush around electrical switch plates.

How to fold a fitted sheet

Folding sheets is an extremely fiddly business, and everyone has a different way of doing it. Here is a clear set of instructions to help make it as straightforward as possible:

1. Take the sheet out of the dryer or off the clothesline and shake it out. Make sure you have it turned so that the long sides of the sheet are across your body.

2. Take one long side and lay it on a flat surface, such as a bed.

3. Pick up the other long side, put your hand inside one of the corners and tuck it into the matching corner of the first side, as if you were pushing your hand into a pair of gloves.

4. Repeat with the other corner. Pick up the sheet. You will have one hand inside one corner and the other hand inside the other corner.

5. Bring one pair of corners to the other and tuck them inside each other. You will now have all four corners together in your right hand. Take the edges together with your left hand and lay it down. Flatten it out and square it off.

6. The fitted end should be to your right and the flat side to your left. Fold over the top so that you have a nice square corner at the top left.

7. Put your hand inside the top right corner and keeping it taut, pull on the top and bottom of the fitted right-hand side, making it as square as possible.

8. Go to the left of the sheet and pull that down to the fitted end. Smooth it out. You'll now have a nice smooth rectangle.

Put your fingers underneath in the middle of the sheet and fold in half. Fold it over one more time if you need to. It will now fit into your linen cupboard and won't look like a fitted sheet at all.

How to iron a shirt

It's best to iron clothing when it is still a bit damp. However, steam irons correct a multitude of sins, especially those that provide a burst of steam and a sprinkle function. Amazingly, it was my father who taught both my mother and me how to iron. I still iron shirts exactly the way he showed me.

Make sure you have a good, stable ironing board and a perfectly clean iron. If you are ironing a new shirt, first try a small area on the inside that doesn't show to make sure the temperature is all right for the fabric.

1. Start with the collar. Place it flat on the board. Iron the inside first, then flip it over and iron the outside.

2. Iron the inside of one cuff, then the outside. Line up the

sleeve on the board, making sure the seam is straight, and press one side. Turn the sleeve over and press the other side. If there are any pleats in the sleeve, press them carefully with the tip of the iron. Repeat with the other sleeve.

3. Laying the shirt out along the length of the ironing board, iron the shoulder panel, then the back of the shirt.

4. Finally, iron the front, pressing the pockets first if there are any, then the button (and buttonhole) panels and, lastly, the front of the shirt.

How to clean a diamond

Diamonds may be a girl's best friend, but only sparkly clean diamonds are beautiful. Here's how to keep yours, no matter how modest, in the best condition.

In a microwaveable bowl, mix one part ammonia to six parts water. Heat to the boil in a microwave oven and boil for two minutes (without the diamond).

Remove the bowl from the oven and put the diamond into the solution. Soak for five to ten minutes.

Put a little washing-up liquid on a clean toothbrush and brush the diamond ring, getting into all the nooks and crannies. Rinse and dry with a soft cloth.

Looking after your pearls

Pearls are very fragile, even cultured ones that have a thick coating of nacre, and they are worth a lot of TLC. (Please note that all of these tips are for wild pearls and cultured pearls. Fake pearls don't count.)

- If you have pearls, wear them often. Some say every day, but that's too restrictive. I assume you have other jewellery you also like.

- Always wear your pearls directly on naked skin.

- Pearls should be the last thing you put on and the first thing you take off. Don't put on your pearls until after you've applied your make-up, perfume and lotions. This will prevent these products from building up on your jewellery.

- Use a soft, lint-free cloth to wipe your pearls after you take them off.

- When not wearing them, keep your pearls in a pouch or wrap to prevent them knocking against other jewellery.

Remedies

Stings and how to treat them

Honeybee stings

Honeybees, with their fuzzy, golden-brown bodies, are very cute and useful creatures, but being stung by one doesn't feel cute at all. The barbed stinger remains embedded in your skin, pumping venom, driving the stinger and its poison deeper and deeper into your skin. It's not great news for the bee either, because after it attacks you, it dies.

The trick is to remove the stinger as quickly as possible. Use your fingernail, a nail file, or even the edge of a credit card to scrape gently underneath the stinger and flip it out. Don't try to grab the stinger with tweezers as you might do with a splinter. This may squeeze more poison into your skin. As soon as you can, clean the area with soap and water or an antiseptic.

Bumblebee and wasp stings

Unlike their cousins the honeybees, bumblebees have smooth stingers, like wasps. They can attack you again and again, so if you get stung once and the creature is still flying around, don't try to kill it or antagonize it, RUN.

But it still hurts! So your next task is to deaden the pain as quickly as possible. There are several ways to do this.

❈ Ice: an ice pack or even a single ice cube placed over the sting will reduce the swelling and keep the venom from spreading.

❈ Heat: this also works. If you have a hairdryer, turn it on and aim it at your sting – but be careful not to burn yourself!

❈ Aspirin: wet the sting, then rub an aspirin tablet into it. But if you are sensitive or allergic to aspirin, forget this one.

❈ Bicarbonate of soda: make a paste with water and apply to the affected area.

❈ Mud: if nothing else is available, a mud paste (just mix with cold water) can soothe a sting. Apply, cover with a bandage, handkerchief or clingfilm and leave on until the mud dries.

Mosquito bites

To deter mosquitoes from taking a bite out of you, instead of slathering yourself with repellent cream you can simply eat foods rich in vitamin B1 – including wholegrain cereals, porridge oats, brown rice, nuts, dairy products and red meat. Or you could simply take supplements of it – your local health store or pharmacy should stock it.

Nettle stings

If you are stung by nettles, your best bet is to wipe any mud or dirt from the area with cold water on a clean cloth. Don't rub too hard or you will irritate the sting even further.

If you know what you are looking for, search for a dock plant, which usually grows around nettles. It has large leaves and a thick stem. Snap off a leaf with a stem and crush the end of the stem to soften it, then rub it on the sting. However, if you know as little about plants as I do, try the following remedies instead:

- Apply any alkaline product to the stung area, such as bicarbonate of soda, cucumber, parsley, celery or lettuce.
- Spit on the affected area, but do not touch it with your mouth. This will only relieve the pain temporarily, but is something that is always available. Rub the spit over the sting with a piece of clean cloth or tissue.

Jellyfish stings

Jellyfish stings come from the long tentacles that trail from the bell-shaped jellyfish. Being stung by a jellyfish or Portuguese man-of-war is very nasty. One of my daughters was stung in the sea in Florida and a quick-thinking neighbour gave me meat tenderizer powder to rub on it. This apparently contains an enzyme called papain, derived from papaya, which deactivates venom protein.

Because some jellyfish are more deadly than others (Indo-Pacific and Australian are the worst), it is best to seek medical attention as quickly as possible, but if this is not practical, rinse the sting with seawater. Do not use fresh water, which will cause more toxins to be released. Remove any remaining tentacles with tweezers or a gloved hand.

At the risk of stating the obvious, the best way to treat jellyfish stings is to prevent them from happening in the first place: don't swim in jellyfish-infested waters.

Reducing the pain of burns

Small but painful burns can be treated either by slitting a vitamin E capsule and applying it to the burnt spot, or breaking off a mature aloe vera leaf and squeezing the gel onto the burn. This is advice for non-serious, first or second-degree burns – but if the skin has blistered and the area is larger than a 10-pence piece or so severe that it doesn't hurt (because the nerve endings have been damaged), the burn requires medical aid.

Getting rid of head lice

Lice are not the end of the world (although we might think they are when we find them, or nits, on our child's hair). Contrary to popular belief, lice will choose a clean human host with clean hair, rather than a grubby child with dirty hair. If your child goes to school, nursery, parties, or anywhere else where there are other children, they may bring home these unwelcome visitors.

Most of the medications available tend to be fairly harsh on the scalp, so you might choose a more natural approach such as mayonnaise or olive oil.

Use a new jar of mayo that hasn't been in the fridge, because that would be way too cold. Cover your child's hair with it, then put a plastic shower cap or plastic bag over the mayo mess to keep it from dripping. Leave this on for two hours, then throw away the plastic cap, wash your and your child's hands and shampoo the hair thoroughly. It may take several shampoos to get the hair clean.

After shampooing, rinse your child's hair and scalp with white vinegar, which will loosen any nits clinging to the hair shafts. Use comfortably hot water. Comb the tangles out with a wide-toothed comb, then comb again with a nit comb, which has very fine teeth. If you find any nits, pick them off and put them into a bowl to which you have added white vinegar or soapy water.

If there are still a reasonable number of nits in the hair, dip a clean towel in a half and half vinegar/water mixture and wrap this around your child's head for another hour. Then shampoo and rinse again as before.

When you've done all that, you must wash all clothing, towels and bedlinen that have come into contact with your child in the previous week in hot water, drying them on the hot cycle if you have a tumble dryer. Hairbrushes, combs, hair ornaments, ponytail holders and the like must either be discarded or soaked in hot vinegar. And furniture and carpets need to be vacuumed thoroughly.

You will have to check your child's hair (and everyone else's who lives with you) daily until you are all clear. And if you have older children, try to impress upon them that they shouldn't borrow or lend combs or hairbrushes.

Dealing with fleas

If you have animals, you will have fleas. For a purely natural route, eucalyptus oil or pennyroyal shampoo works, as do natural herb powders. And if your animals will accept them, garlic and brewer's yeast tablets absolutely disgust fleas. However, if the fleas persist, go to your vet for something stronger.

Plants, herbs and spices that heal

Plants, herbs and spices are valuable for much more than just cookery. Keen gardeners have used herbs to heal common ailments from time immemorial. While medical advice should always be sought for serious ailments, these natural remedies do work a treat on minor ones. Of course, if you are already on any prescribed medication, it's a good idea to check with your pharmacist before taking any of the following. Here are some of the more common options:

Aloe Vera: this will grow beautifully on your window-sill and the gel inside the mature leaves is a good remedy for burns of all sorts.

Chamomile: usually used for tea, this has a soothing effect on the digestive system and can calm minor skin problems.

Echinacea: boosts the immune system and staves off colds. If you should get a cold, echinacea will often lessen the severity and duration.

Garlic: not only an aid to keep vampires away, garlic is also great for preventing and easing the symptoms of the common cold and coughs.

Ginger: is supposed to aid circulation. I also think it helps nausea, so I always have a jar of crystallized ginger to hand.

Lavender oil: has a broad range of healing properties. It is an antiseptic, which makes it an excellent general cleaning agent when diluted in warm water. It is also one of the few essential oils that can be applied directly to the skin undiluted, and is used widely in aromatherapy. If you are feeling anxious, picking a clump of lavender, crushing it in your hands and inhaling the scent will help to calm you down.

St John's wort: is a natural remedy to treat mild depression and 'the blues'. But it does have side effects so only take this under advice.

Tea tree oil: is very versatile and is used for various purposes owing to its antiseptic and antifungal properties.

Valerian: insomnia is often caused by anxiety and valerian has been known to set the scene for calm and restful sleep.

Toothache

It goes without saying that if you have a toothache, you should make an appointment with your dentist without delay. But when it happens on a Sunday or public holiday this might not be an option, so it is a good idea to keep a little bottle of oil of cloves in your medicine cabinet for such emergencies. You can buy it at your pharmacist without a prescription.

Oil of cloves contains a large amount of the anaesthetic and antiseptic chemical eugenol. Dentists use it as a pain-reliever and it is safe and effective for temporary use on a tooth that throbs. It should be placed directly on the tooth, not ingested.

If you haven't got any oil of cloves, try this: boil one part sesame seeds with two parts water until the liquid is reduced by half. Apply it to the aching tooth. The reason it works is because sesame contains at least seven pain-relieving compounds.

Eat your parsley

The sprig of parsley that often garnishes your plate is more than just a pretty decoration – it is also very good for you. It can freshen your breath; my mother maintained that it is good for the nerves, and she enjoyed munching it. There is some scientific evidence to support what I had always thought of as an 'old wives' tale'. Apparently the nutrients in parsley are powerfully therapeutic for the optic nerves, the brain and the whole sympathetic nervous system.

Headaches and migraines

These are commonplace complaints, and if you are a regular sufferer from either, it can be extremely debilitating. In both instances it is wise to avoid caffeine, chocolate, cheese, citrus fruits and alcohol. It is also wise to prevent your blood sugar levels dropping low by eating little and often rather than just having three heavy meals a day. Foods rich in vitamin E are beneficial for headache sufferers (nuts, various vegetable oils, muesli and avocados), while ginger either in food or as a drink is supposed to alleviate migraines.

Natural old-fashioned remedies

This is by no means an exhaustive list of home remedies; they include only those either I or my family have personally tried and found to be effective.

Athlete's foot

The best way to cure athlete's foot is to go barefoot. Fungi multiply in damp environments and shoes and socks exacerbate moistness. Going barefoot may not be very practical in the middle of the winter so – since moisture and darkness are the culprits – sprinkling sodium bicarbonate into your shoes (and socks) will help. Sprinkling cider vinegar into shoes also works well because it is a natural antiseptic.

Bad breath

Sucking on a clove will sweeten your breath, but a very powerful solution is cardamom, which is a potent antiseptic. Just chew the seeds (which are also purported to be a potent aphrodisiac).

Biting your tongue

A surprisingly common problem this! A used, wet teabag on the bitten part of the tongue works wonders to ease the pain.

Bladder infections and cystitis

A traditional method for both treating and staving off

bladder infections is drinking cranberry juice. But you have to drink a lot of it – more than you would probably like. Cranberry tablets work quicker and better. If the discomfort persists you must see your doctor.

Eating yogurt is another good remedy, but it has to be live yogurt with 'friendly' bacteria to do any good.

Body odour

If you are allergic to commercial deodorants or would like to solve the body odour problem in a more natural way, mix sodium bicarbonate and cornflour together and dust your armpits with it. It is fragrance-free and effective. White vinegar also works since it is an antiseptic, but the idea of dousing myself in it doesn't appeal to me.

Bruises

Arnica – either the little homeopathic pillules you put on your tongue from the dispenser (without touching them with your fingers) or the cream – is wonderful for bruises.

Flatulence

Everyone experiences flatulence from time to time, and one major culprit is eating beans. However, if you are planning a dish using dried beans, soak them in water overnight, discard that water and cook them in new water, and you will find that this helps enormously. And an old folk remedy – cooking a carrot with the beans – is another anti-gas strategy. I don't know what the science is, but it works.

Hangovers

A good way of preventing hangovers is to follow the old maxim 'Don't mix the grape and the grain', but if it's too late for that, the most important thing to do is rehydrate. So, first things first, drink lots of water. Traditionally, a breakfast of eggs has always been recommended – and science confirms this as sage advice because of the amino acid cysteine found in eggs, which helps to break down the toxins from the alcohol.

Hiccups

One teaspoon (5ml) of cider vinegar stirred into a glass of warm water will usually cure annoying hiccups.

Motion sickness and nausea

You can purchase all sorts of medication and even gadgets to guard against motion sickness and nausea, but I think you will find that ginger works very well. It doesn't matter whether the ginger is raw, crystallized or in ginger ale. We gave our children ginger ale if they were sick and it always worked. Another remedy that doesn't seem to be popular, or even widely available, is cola syrup, but cola drinks are pretty effective.

Mouth ulcers (canker sores)

Some people seem to have a recurring problem with mouth ulcers, which are painful and uncomfortable and are sometimes caused when you are stressed or run down. Two very effective solutions are eating plain live yogurt every day and applying a wet, but not hot, ordinary teabag to the ulcer as a sort of compress.

Sinus problems

People who have sinus problems often suffer from headaches as well as stuffed noses. A friend of mine swears by horseradish, which she grows in her garden. If you are brave, you can grate it and eat it on its own, or use it in recipes, for example add it to soup, or even just sniff it.

Sore throat

Vinegar kills bacteria so for a sore throat just mix 1 part honey to 1 part cider vinegar and take 1 tablespoonful (15ml) four times a day.

Gargling with salt water is another effective remedy for sore throats and gum problems (but the cause of the gum problems should be investigated with your dentist).

Another sore throat/cough remedy is much more palatable and works just as well. Mix 1 part honey, 1 part whisky or vodka and 1 part lemon juice. Heat in a small saucepan until almost boiling. Cool, then take 1 tablespoonful (15ml) as needed up to four times a day. Children can be given the mixture without the booze – just honey and lemon.

Food and Cooking: The Basics

Shopping for food

What are the best places to shop for food? Difficult question. Ideally, the best place for you to shop is the place where you get the freshest food with the least waste, but often with our busy lives the best place is simply the one that is the most geographically convenient. It's always worth researching to see if there is a local market or farmer's market in your area – it is a good way to support your local community, and you will usually be able to get much fresher, tastier food there.

Here are some handy tips to remember before heading out to do your weekly shop:

※ It is a well-documented fact that you should never go food shopping when you are hungry because you will buy more than you intended. Also, you shouldn't shop if you are angry, lonely or tired.

- If you can shop without your children, you will not have to deal with items being smuggled surreptitiously into your trolley, or tantrums when you say they can't have something they are clutching. Take your family's preferences into consideration when you are making your list at home, not in the grocery aisle.

- You should always shop with a list. It can be fairly basic to allow for special offers, for instance, 'fruit, veg, bread, milk, coffee, fish, meat, cheese, butter, sugar'. If there are any recipes you want to prepare, the ingredients for those should be added, with quantities of what you will need. Nothing is more frustrating than to go to the store with a list that includes an item such as chicken breasts or rhubarb without any idea how much is required.

Sometimes buying more is economical. Say, for instance, you see a beautiful joint of meat at the butcher's and you figure it's twice as big (and twice as expensive) as you would ordinarily buy. But if it provides you with more than twice as many meals that you will enjoy eating, it's worth it if you can afford it.

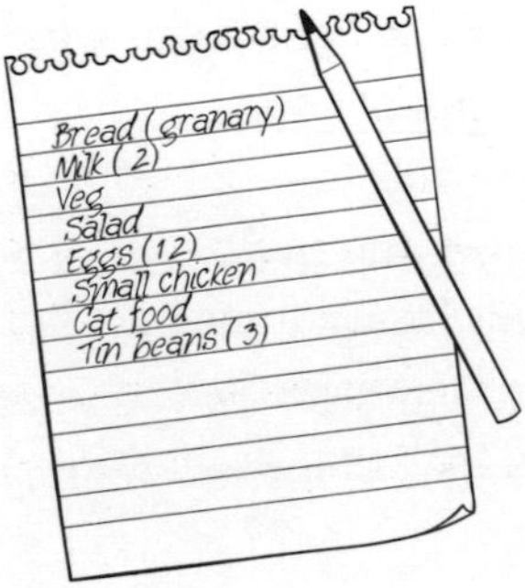

Keeping salad and soft fruit fresh

Take a supermarket plastic punnet – the sort that plums and peaches come in – and line with two sheets of kitchen paper. Tip the unused salad in, cover with two more sheets and enclose the punnet in a plastic bag – the green vegetable saver kind if possible, otherwise an ordinary freezer-type bag. Store in the fridge in the vegetable compartment.

For soft fruit you can use the plastic punnet it came in, lining it top and bottom with kitchen paper before replacing the lid.

Skinning and deseeding fruit and vegetables

Obviously some fruit and vegetables can easily be peeled: potatoes, carrots, parsnips, pumpkin, squash, apples and pears come to mind.

Others, such as tomatoes, plums and peaches, are trickier and need to be skinned. To skin a tomato (or a peach or plum), put it in a bowl and cover with boiling water. After a minute or so, transfer it to a work surface and nick the skin. You will then be able to remove all the skin in large pieces, just by grabbing it and peeling it back with your fingers. To remove the seeds from a tomato, either cut into quarters and cut them out (if the shape matters), or if you will be cooking it, just squeeze! Isn't that simple?

If the skin of a pepper needs to be charred, this is best done on top of a gas hob. Just lay the pepper on a medium flame. After a couple of minutes, turn it over. When the skin is charred all over, lift it with a large spoon into a bowl and cover with clingfilm. Leave to cool. You can then pick all the skin off easily. To remove the seeds, cut off the stem end, slice the pepper in half vertically and push the seeds out with the flat side of a knife.

Get more juice out of citrus fruit

When you shop for lemons (or any other citrus fruit), what you should buy depends on how you are going to use them. If you want pretty, quartered or sliced lemons for garnish, buy the oval, shiny yellow fruits with thick skins.

But if you want juice, these will not produce it. What you need in this case are those ugly, small, round lemons. They have almost no skin, so are almost all juice.

Before you juice them, bring them up to room temperature or drop into a bowl of warm water – or pop them into the microwave on high for about ten seconds. Roll them around on the countertop to release the juice, then squeeze.

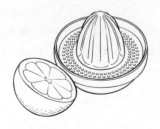

Keep salt flowing freely

If you use a salt shaker rather than grinding it, you will find that it flows much more freely if you put a few grains of raw rice in the shaker before you fill it. The rice will absorb any moisture in the container and you won't have to bang the shaker on the table before you use it.

Opening a jar

Mostly everyone has a favourite method for opening a jar. All of the following usually work:

❀ Give it to a man, bat your eyelashes and say, 'Could you open this for me please?'

❀ Insert a small spoon between the lid and the jar to break the vacuum.

❀ Put a rubber band (like the ones you find on asparagus and throw into your kitchen junk drawer) around the lid and turn – this will give you more traction.

❀ Turn the jar upside down and tap it lightly on the kitchen countertop, then turn it back upright and the jar will now open.

- Hold the jar's rim under hot water.
- If you have a pair of rubber gloves, put them on and turn the lid.

Cookery tips

Good cooking does not require any special talent. All that's needed is quality ingredients (you can't make a silk purse out of a sow's ear), a little time and the ability to read a recipe. You must read the recipe all the way through and check that you have all the ingredients. You should also read the method to make sure you understand what you have to do.

- When cooking the main meal of the day or when baking, collect all of the ingredients you need and put them on the worktop. If you need to do any advance preparation, such as marinating or preheating the oven, do so. After you have used each ingredient, put it aside.
- The first time you make a recipe, use the exact measurements. You can always tweak it next time if you are not entirely happy, but under-measure the salt (unless you are baking bread where the yeast and salt have to be in the correct ratio).

✼ If you are cooking one thing in the oven at a specific temperature and think you want to cook something else along with it that specifies a different temperature, don't – at least not if you are a novice cook. If your main dish is going into the oven, cook the vegetables either on top of the hob or in the microwave if you have one. Don't try to juggle too many recipes at one time or they won't come out right.

✼ If you are entertaining and are new to it, don't be too ambitious. Make a really easy starter – either something you can prepare in advance or a salad that only requires arranging. For the main course, cook something you have done successfully in the past that doesn't involve too much of your time in the kitchen when your guests arrive. Dessert can be a simple cheeseboard with fruit or bought ice cream or sorbet, or forget dessert and serve nice chocolates or biscuits with coffee or tea.

Food hygiene

When storing and handling food, follow these basic hygiene guidelines to help guard against food poisoning.

❀ When preparing food, always start with clean hands.

❀ Raw food needs to be separated from cooked food because of potential cross-contamination, when bacteria spreads from the raw items to the cooked.

❀ Fresh raw meat, poultry and seafood should be stored on the bottom shelf of the fridge on a plate so that the juices can't drip onto other foods. Chill as soon as possible after bringing the food home and ensure that your freezer and refrigerator are operating at optimum temperatures.

❀ Everyone recommends using one cutting board for raw meat, poultry and seafood and another for foods that are ready to eat, such as salads and fruit. What is important in my opinion is to keep the cutting board scrupulously clean. Hot soapy water and a good scrub with sodium bicarbonate each time it is used works for me.

❀ Never put cooked food onto a plate that has previously held uncooked meat, poultry or seafood without washing it thoroughly first.

⌘ When you are cooking food, ensure that you are heating it to a safe temperature. This is particularly important for leftover sauces, soups and stews – in fact, anything that is being reheated. I like my beef rare and buy good-quality meat, so I'll take my chances. But never, *never* undercook poultry.

Cooking with kids

When my children came along, I let them help me from a very early age. It gave them a connection with food and how it is prepared. If you grow some of your own vegetables and fruit, let the children or grandchildren help pick them and, if applicable, let them taste them raw – for instance, tomatoes, green beans, carrots, peas. Then let them help you prepare meals according to their ability and confidence. I'm a keen baker, and this piqued my childrens' interest.

Sometimes they will make a mess. Sometimes they will make a mistake. But it's a good fun way of spending time together, and if they persevere, they'll thank you for it when they grow up.

Fishy odours

A good way to eliminate the fishy odour from your kitchen is to pour some white vinegar into a bowl, place it on the kitchen worktop and leave it for a few hours. The smell will disappear.

Oversalting

One common cooking disaster is adding too much salt, by misreading teaspoons for tablespoons, for instance. Don't panic and throw all those good ingredients away. Your best bet is to add more vegetables or tomato or vegetable juice. If, after all your ministrations, it is still too salty, you *will* have to admit defeat and bin it.

If your oversalted dish is uncooked, you will need to be creative. A salad could always use more salad leaves.

How to stretch meals

If you are planning dinner for one or two and your siblings and best friend show up just before dinnertime (hopefully not all at once), that's what I would call bad manners. If this happens regularly, you're either a terrific cook or you need to have a chat with these people.

Nevertheless, you can still be gracious and invite them to eat with you if you have these ingredients on hand: dried pasta, tinned tomatoes, fresh or longlife milk, rice, eggs and cheese. Leftover vegetables, meat, fish and poultry can also be an asset. Keep these essentials in your store cupboard or fridge and you will have the basis for a pasta casserole, a risotto, an omelette or frittata. You can look at some sample recipes in the recipe section on pages 71–97.

Creative leftovers

When my children lived at home, I went through a phase of cleaning out my fridge and making the contents into a sort of stew that we would have on Sunday. This stew consisted of any meat or poultry, rice, pasta and potatoes that had been cooked during the week, plus any raw or cooked vegetables. The only thing that never got included was fish. This was quite fun in the beginning, but it got very samey and the children got bored, so I stopped.

Nowadays I sometimes still cook for an army – old habits are hard to break – but the very large boneless pork roast that is my favourite joint will produce an original roasted dinner for four to six, plus delicious Sunday night sandwiches, a stir-fry, a casserole and a pasta bake at the very least. I find that if I slice or cube it as I need it, the meat remains succulent to the tasty end.

The fish (that didn't go into the stew) usually gets labelled and frozen and makes wonderful fishcakes.

Leftover risotto, potatoes, noodles and pasta plus some vegetable odds and ends and cheese make delicious frittatas.

Bread too stale for sandwiches becomes croutons for salads and soup and breadcrumbs to coat fish and poultry and top casseroles.

Fruit and berries frequently get puréed and frozen to be made into sorbets, ice cream and coulis at some later date. Vegetables sometimes get puréed as well and are used to augment soup or flesh out a sauce.

Cooking with eggs

Testing eggs for freshness

A really fresh egg from a happy hen is a joy to eat, but how can you tell how fresh your eggs are? If you keep chickens, it's easy. When you collect your eggs, just write the date you gathered them on the egg with a soft pencil, being careful not to crack the shell.

If you buy eggs, make sure you use them before the 'best by' date. But this date could be twenty-eight days after they are laid – not exactly what I would call a 'fresh' egg. Also, many people don't store their eggs in cartons, so again, unless you write on every egg, you won't have a clue.

There is a simple way you can test for freshness: fill a deep bowl with cold water. Gently submerge the egg. If it sinks to the bottom of the bowl and lays on its side, it is fresh. If it sinks and stands upright, it's a few days old. But beware if it floats, because this is a sure sign of a rotten egg.

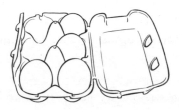

Storing eggs

Store your eggs in the carton or on an egg tree in a cool area of your kitchen. Place them pointed end down, broad end up. Kept this way, they will stay fresh for several weeks. If you are at all unsure about them, do the test above.

Eggs don't need to be kept in a refrigerator unless your home is very hot – but if you must, they should never be stored in an egg keeper in the door as this is furthest away from the cooling mechanism and the temperature fluctuates every time the door is opened. Leave them in their carton in the fridge, eliminating the possibility of fridge odours permeating them.

Separating an egg

The plastic egg separators sold in kitchen shops are a waste of time and money. All you need are bowls – two if you are separating one egg and three if you have to separate several.

Crack the egg sharply in the centre on a kitchen worktop or cutting board. Over one of the bowls, prise the eggshell apart with your thumbs, letting the yolk rest in the lower half of the shell, allowing the white to fall into the bowl. Carefully transfer the egg yolk back and forth between the shells until all that is in the shell is yolk. Drop that into the second bowl.

For each subsequent egg, use the third bowl to collect the egg white, making sure not even a drop of yolk gets in. Then you can pour that egg white into the first bowl. In this way, if any of the yolks is broken, you will not be contaminating a bowlful of egg whites with even the teeniest bit of yolk – worth washing another bowl for! And if a bit of eggshell should find its way into the whites, just fish it out with a larger piece of eggshell.

Using leftover egg whites

If you find yourself with a surplus of egg whites, no problem. They can eventually be made into meringues or used to lighten cake batters. Weigh the whites and place in a freezer container marked with the weight and the date you are freezing. Use within six months. A typical large egg white weighs approximately 40g (1½oz).

Using leftover egg yolks

Extra egg yolks can be put in a small covered container in the fridge if you will be using them within a few days. You can also freeze them by weighing and marking as above. If you will be using them for sweet dishes, you can add a pinch of sugar. If you are not sure, don't! Egg yolks have the same freezer life as egg whites. A typical large egg yolk weighs about 20g (¾oz).

Recipes

The perfect poached egg

Some cooking 'tricks' have come down through the ages, but this is a modern take on an old classic – the poached egg. I learned this tip from the internet and it works perfectly every time. I have told lots of people about it and they agree. One friend texted me to say she was just tucking into one and considering making another because it was so good!

Line a ramekin with a piece of microwaveable non-PVC clingfilm large enough to wrap around the egg. Crack the egg into the lined cup and secure the clingfilm around the egg with a twist tie.

Once you've done this, boil enough water in a saucepan to cover the egg, then remove the tied egg from the ramekin, drop into the boiling water and simmer as usual. Depending on the size of the eggs and whether you like your eggs runny or firm, leave to simmer for between three to six minutes. It comes out neat and perfect and you won't have to scrub cooked-on egg off the pan. No fuss, no muss. You can poach as many eggs as your saucepan will hold in one layer.

Omelette

Making an omelette is really as easy as breaking the eggs. You just need a well-seasoned frying pan that has been lovingly looked after.

Serves 2–4

You will need (per person):
2 large eggs
1–2 tbsp cream, milk or water
1 tbsp butter
Handful of chopped parsley or other herbs
Salt and freshly ground black pepper
Optional ingredients:
Grated cheese, sausages, bacon, chicken, fresh tomatoes, mushrooms, olives

1. In a bowl, beat the eggs together with the cream, milk or water.

2. Set your frying pan over a medium heat. When it is hot, melt the butter, then pour in the egg mixture, add the herbs and season with salt and pepper. Using a spatula, lift the mixture from the sides and allow the uncooked egg to pour underneath.

3. Sprinkle evenly with your optional ingredients. At this point I like to put the omelette in the oven or under the grill to heat everything up, cook the top and melt the cheese. If you are doing this and your frying-pan handle is wood, cover it with aluminium foil before placing it in the oven.

4. To serve, cut into wedges or fold over and cut into portions.

Rice frittata

This is a very nice way of serving leftover rice. If you use a frying pan with a wooden handle, remember to wrap the handle in aluminium foil before putting in the oven in step 4.

Serves: depends how hungry you are

You will need:
2 eggs, mixed with a little water, milk or cream
A cupful or so of cooked rice
3 very large mushrooms, sliced or chopped

For the topping:
Chopped parsley
Cheddar cheese
Freshly ground pepper
Fresh or dried herbs, for example thyme or oregano
(optional)

1. Preheat the oven to 180°C (350°F/Gas Mark 4).

2. Make an omelette with the eggs, lifting the edges as it cooks to let the uncooked egg flow underneath.

3. Remove the frying-pan from the heat. Spread the rice evenly over the top of the omelette, then scatter the mushrooms. Sprinkle with parsley and cheese. Season with pepper and add herbs if using. Flatten the topping with a spatula.

4. Place the pan in the oven and cook until the cheese melts and bubbles, about five minutes. Remove from the oven, cut into wedges and serve with salad.

Homemade croutons

There's a limit to the amount of stale bread you can use to feed the local ducks – but you don't have to waste it by throwing it away. Make the bread into breadcrumbs for coating and topping, or follow the recipe below to turn it into croutons for soup and salad.

It doesn't matter what kind of bread you use. Anything you can slice and cut into cubes works. It's best to make only as much as you need unless your bread is in danger of becoming a penicillin plant. In that case, cut into cubes and freeze in plastic bags or whizz into breadcrumbs and freeze.

When you are ready to make the croutons, line a baking sheet with aluminium foil. Preheat the oven to 180°C (350°F/Gas Mark 4). Lay the bread cubes on the foil in one layer, sprinkle with olive oil and season with salt and pepper, and garlic and herbs if you like. Bake for about 15–20 minutes, turning the cubes once halfway through the cooking time, when they are golden brown and dry. If they are in danger of browning too much, turn down the temperature and cover with foil.

The vinaigrette ratio

There's really no need to buy commercial salad dressing when it is so easy to make your own. Here are some ideas:

Basic vinaigrette

Most people use a 3:1 ratio for oil and vinegar, but this is all about personal taste so you must experiment. Use the best olive oil you can afford. You can substitute nut oil (walnut, hazelnut, macadamia nut) for some of the olive oil if you like. The quantities below are suggestions – you can increase or decrease them as you like.

> You will need:
> 6 tbsp extra virgin olive oil
> 2 tbsp vinegar (dark or white balsamic, sherry, raspberry or rice)
> Optional (to taste):
> 2 tsp freshly squeezed lemon juice
> Pinch of mustard powder
> Chopped fresh or dried herbs
> Pinch of salt and freshly ground black pepper

Put the olive oil and vinegar into a screwtop jar and stir. If it tastes too bland, add the lemon juice and taste again. Then add whatever seasonings you prefer.

Basic no-fat vinaigrette

You will need:
3 parts orange juice
1 part white balsamic vinegar
1 tsp dried Italian herbs
Pinch of salt and freshly ground black pepper

Put everything into a screwtop jar and shake. You can use the dressing immediately, but it is really better to make it beforehand and then store it in the refrigerator to allow the flavours to blend.

Pasta casserole

You can put almost anything you like in this casserole. If you are a vegetarian, just leave out the chicken, fish or meat. This recipe gives you an idea of what you can use. Any ingredient can be omitted or added. It's just a matter of taste.

Serves 2–4

You will need:
250g (9oz) dry pasta of your choice (spaghetti, linguine, penne, shells, etc.)
About 600ml (1 pint) sauce, such as béchamel, stockcube based or wine/tomato
Optional ingredients:
Leftover cubed cooked chicken or meat or cooked prawns, shrimp, flaked crayfish or white fish

Olives, stoned and sliced if large
Mushrooms, sautéed in a little olive oil
Cooked vegetables cut into bite-sized pieces
Chopped tinned tomatoes or halved cherry tomatoes

For the topping:
Grated cheese
Breadcrumbs

1. Preheat the oven to 180°C (350°F/Gas Mark 4). Grease a 23 x 30cm (9 x 12in) baking dish.

2. Cook the pasta until *al dente* and drain.

3. Make the sauce or heat it up.

4. Pour the sauce and pasta in the baking dish and add the chicken, meat or fish, and olives, mushrooms and vegetables, if you are using.

5. Top with the tomatoes, scatter with the cheese and breadcrumbs and bake until the cheese melts and the sauce bubbles, about 15 minutes. Remove from the oven and serve hot.

Fishcakes

You can create a lovely supper using leftover cooked white fish or salmon or a combination of both. The only caveat is that the seasonings in whatever you choose should be compatible. Wrap the fish leftovers first in parchment paper and then in foil, label the packet with the weight and store it in the freezer. When you have a sufficient number of packets, you can make fishcakes. If you don't have any leftover fish, use tinned yellowfin tuna instead – it's also very good. You can use either mashed potato or breadcrumbs as the filler, and a bit of mashed root vegetable adds a little interest as well. My measurements are approximate since you can't really figure how much you are going to have left over. This will give you an idea.

Makes about 4 good-sized fishcakes

You will need:
350g (12oz) leftover cooked fish, thawed if frozen
2 eggs
Homemade breadcrumbs or mashed potato (about half the volume of the fish, which works out at about a cupful of either)
Leftover mashed root vegetables
Chopped fresh parsley or dill
Salt and freshly ground black pepper
Breadcrumbs, for coating
Paprika or ground cumin or both to sprinkle
Butter and olive oil or nut oil, for frying

1. Put the fish into a bowl and flake with a fork.

2. Whisk the eggs in a cup and add to the fish, then start adding the breadcrumbs or potato. Mix, adding any vegetables as well, and the parsley or dill. Season with salt and pepper. When the mixture is sufficiently firm, form it into balls.

3. Take a sheet of parchment paper and lay it on the worktop. Pour a small quantity of breadcrumbs on the paper. Taking one ball at a time, lay it on the crumbs and flatten it into a cake. Turn over and coat the other side. When you have done all the cakes, take them, paper and all, and put on a plate. Season the tops with paprika and/ or cumin. Chill the fishcakes in the refrigerator for at least 30 minutes to firm them up.

4. When ready to cook, melt a little butter and oil in a large frying pan. Slide a spatula under each fishcake and put it, spiced side down, in the pan. Sprinkle a bit more spice on top and cook for 5 minutes over a medium heat. Turn the fishcakes over and cook for a further 5 minutes until golden brown.

5. Serve hot with salad, vegetables or boiled potatoes. I usually serve mine with a dollop of sweet chilli sauce on the plate, but you can make a herb béchamel if you prefer.

Everything-in-the-fridge stew

This is a great solution if you want to serve up leftover vegetables and meat in a new way, and certainly goes down well with the family!

Serves as many as necessary

Combine the leftovers in a stewpot with some cubed, cooked potatoes, cooked rice or pasta and whatever stock you fancy, plus a glass of wine. You can also add some fresh carrots, parsnips, onions and mushrooms, which you have microwaved. Bring the contents of the pot to the boil, reduce the heat and simmer to heat through thoroughly. Taste and season if necessary, then serve with crusty bread.

Risotto

You can add any vegetable, meat, fish or herb to this risotto at the very end. This is just the basic recipe that I use.

Serves 2–4

You will need:
900ml (1½ pints) vegetable, chicken or meat stock (depending on what else you are planning to add or what is available)
2 tbsp olive oil
Couple of shallots or chopped onion
225g (8oz) arborio or carnaroli rice
Small wineglass of dry white wine
1 tbsp grated Parmesan cheese
1 tbsp double cream (optional)
Additional ingredients, as liked (see introduction), cut into bite-sized pieces

1. Put the stock into a saucepan and bring to a simmer.

2. In another saucepan, heat the olive oil over a medium heat and sweat the shallots or onion for a few minutes. Add the rice and stir for about 2 minutes.

3. Pour in the wine. When it has reduced to almost nothing, start adding the simmering stock, a ladleful at a time. Turn the heat down if it is bubbling fast. Stir until the first ladleful of stock is absorbed, then add another ladleful. Keep stirring and set your kitchen timer for 20

minutes. You might not need to add all the stock. Taste after 20 minutes. If it is creamy and *al dente*, it is done.

4. Stir in the cheese and cream, if using, then add your chosen ingredients. Reheat, stirring for a moment, then remove from the heat and cover the saucepan with a lid. Serve piping hot.

Steak rub

You can make your own almost as easily as buying a ready-made rub, so my rule of thumb is to do it yourself. The rub will taste fresher, too.

You will need:
1 tsp ground cumin
1 tsp chilli powder
2 tsp salt
1 tsp freshly ground black pepper
½ tsp cayenne pepper
2 tsp finely chopped shallots
1½ tsp light or dark brown sugar

Combine the ingredients in a small bowl. Rub all over the steaks and set aside to allow the flavours to permeate the meat. Then cook your steak as you like it. Store the leftover rub in a labelled spice jar.

Chicken good enough for a dinner party

This deceptively simple recipe will bring you rave reviews. You can then spend more time making a wicked dessert!

Serves 6

You will need:
675g (1½lb) cherry tomatoes
4 tbsp olive oil, plus extra for greasing
6 garlic cloves, crushed
1½ tsp crushed dried chillies (or more or less to taste)
3 tbsp chopped fresh marjoram or 1½ tbsp dried
6 free-range chicken breasts, with skin and ribs
Salt and freshly ground black pepper

1. Preheat the oven to 230°C (450°F/Gas Mark 8).

2. In a bowl, toss the tomatoes, olive oil, garlic, chillies and half the marjoram. Arrange the chicken breasts in a greased baking dish and pour the tomato mixture over, arranging them in a single layer around the chicken. Season with salt and pepper.

3. Roast until the chicken is cooked right through and the tomatoes are blistered, about 35 minutes.

4. To serve, arrange a chicken breast on each plate. Spoon the tomatoes and juices over the chicken and garnish with the remaining marjoram.

Microwave lemon curd

Try this and you will never buy lemon curd ever again!

Makes 360g (13oz)

You will need:
75g (3oz) unsalted butter, softened
175g (6oz) caster sugar
2 tsp grated lemon zest
60ml (4 tbsp) freshly squeezed lemon juice
3 large eggs, beaten

1. Melt the butter in a saucepan then pour it in a bowl and whisk in the sugar, lemon zest and lemon juice. Add the eggs and blend well.

2. Cover with parchment paper and microwave on high for 3 minutes, stirring well after each minute.

3. Pour into sterilized jam jars and leave to cool. Store in the refrigerator.

VARIATION

For orange or lime curd, substitute appropriate fruit rind and juice. Proceed as directed.

Homemade baking powder

Makes about 6 tablespoons

You will need:
4 tbsp cream of tartar
2 tbsp bicarbonate of soda

Place the cream of tartar and bicarbonate in a fine sieve and sift three times into a small bowl. Store in an airtight container at room temperature. You can keep this mixture for a month, but resift before each use because it tends to clump after it has been stored. Use it as you would commercial baking powder.

Homemade vanilla essence

You will need:
1 empty jam jar with a tight-fitting lid
3 vanilla pods
240ml (8fl oz) white rum or vodka

1. Pour boiling water into the jam jar, allow to rest for 10 minutes to sterilize it and pour out the water.

2. With a sharp knife, slice the vanilla pods lengthways to expose the seeds. Put the pods into the empty jar and add the rum or vodka. Screw the cap on the jar, shake it

a few times and store in a cool, dark cupboard. Label the jar so you remember what's in it.

3. Leave the mixture to steep for about 8 weeks, shaking it occasionally. It will darken during this time.

4. After 8 weeks, the essence is ready. Use however much you need. When you start running low, say, when you've used one-quarter of the essence, top it up with more spirits and give it another shake.

5. If you have used a vanilla pod in a recipe, rinse it off and add it to the essence. If you continue to feed it in this way, it will keep forever. Discard some of the older pods if the jar becomes too crowded.

VARIATION

You can also put rinsed and dried vanilla pods into a bowl of sugar to make your own vanilla sugar.

Courgette tea cake

This is a wholesome, moist and delicious cake. Don't tell the children that it has vegetables in it!

Makes two 900g (2lb) loaves

You will need:
3 large eggs
450g (1lb) golden caster sugar
4–6 medium-sized (15–20cm/6–8in) courgettes, unpeeled and shredded in a food processor
240ml (8fl oz) sunflower, rapeseed or corn oil
2 tsp vanilla essence
2 tsp finely grated orange or lemon zest
275g (10oz) plain flour
50g (2oz) wheatgerm or bran
1 tsp salt
1 tsp bicarbonate of soda
1 tsp baking powder
2 tsp ground cinnamon
1 tsp grated nutmeg
110g (4oz) seedless raisins or dried cranberries
110g (4oz) chopped pecans, walnuts or hazelnuts

1. Preheat the oven to 180°C (350°F /Gas Mark 4). Grease two 900g (2lb) loaf tins or line with baking-parchment loaf-tin liners.

2. In a large bowl, whisk eggs until foamy. Add the sugar, courgettes, oil, vanilla essence and orange or lemon zest and combine well.

3. In another bowl, combine the flour, wheatgerm or bran, salt, bicarbonate of soda, baking powder, cinnamon and nutmeg. Add to the courgette mixture, mixing with a wooden spoon just until ingredients are moistened. Do not overmix.

4. Fold in the raisins or cranberries and nuts and pour evenly into the prepared tins.

5. Bake in the oven for 1 hour 15 minues or until a wooden toothpick inserted into the centre comes out clean. Then remove from the oven and cool in the tins for 10 minutes. Turn out onto wire racks and leave to cool completely.

6. When completely cool, wrap in clingfilm and aluminium foil. They may also be frozen.

Very easy raspberry ice cream

Serves 6–8

You will need:
300g (11oz) fresh raspberries
150g (5oz) caster sugar
2 tbsp framboise (raspberry liqueur) or raspberry syrup
450g (1lb) mascarpone cheese
2 pieces of stem ginger, drained from syrup and
finely chopped
110g (4oz) good-quality plain chocolate, chopped into
very small chunks
Extra berries and chocolate sauce, to serve (optional)

1. Put the raspberries in a bowl and sprinkle with the sugar and framboise or syrup. Leave for half an hour at room temperature until the sugar has dissolved and the raspberries have softened and released a puddle of juice.

2. In another bowl mix together the mascarpone cheese, ginger and chocolate, then swirl the raspberry mixture through.

3. Line a 900g (2lb) loaf tin with clingfilm, leaving lots of overhang, spoon the mixture into the tin, ensuring that the clingfilm covers it. Freeze overnight.

4. To serve, remove from the freezer and lift the ice cream out of the tin using the clingfilm as handles. Cut into slices and transfer to dessert plates. Garnish with extra berries and chocolate sauce, if desired.

Forgotten meringues

This is the treat my grandson always hopes to get at my house.

Makes a lot (about 100)

You will need:
3 large egg whites (about 6 tbsp)
Pinch of salt
175g (6oz) caster sugar
1 tsp vanilla essence
175g (6oz) pecans
175g (6oz) plain chocolate chips

1. Preheat the oven to 180°C (350°F/Gas Mark 4). Line two baking sheets with parchment paper.

2. In a large bowl, whisk the egg whites with the salt until stiff. Gradually whisk in the sugar, little by little, to make a glossy meringue. Gently fold in the vanilla essence, pecans and chocolate chips with a large metal spoon. Spoon heaped teaspoonsful of the mixture onto the prepared baking sheets, spacing them well apart. Put the meringue sheets into the oven and turn the oven off.

3. Leave meringues for 8 hours or overnight and do not open the oven – not even a little peek!

4. Remove from the oven and carefully peel the meringues away from the parchment. Store in an airtight tin, separating the layers with parchment paper.

Mixed berry breakfast cake

No mixed reviews here – it tastes great no matter what you throw in it – dried berries, nuts, any flavour fruit yogurt. I have probably made it a hundred times and everyone raves every time. This is one of its incarnations.

Makes one 25cm (10in) tube cake

You will need:
225g (8oz) sunflower margarine
600g (1lb 5oz) caster sugar
2 tsp vanilla essence
4 large eggs
450g (1lb) plain flour
2 tsp baking powder
1 tsp bicarbonate of soda
1 tsp salt
450g (1lb) vanilla yogurt
175g (6oz) chopped pecans
75g (3oz) dried cranberries or mixed dried berries
2 tsp ground cinnamon

For the topping (optional):
Icing sugar mixed with enough cranberry or lemon juice
    to spread thinly on top

1. Preheat the oven to 180°C (350°F/Gas Mark 4). Lightly grease a 25cm (10in) tube tin.

2. In a large mixing bowl, whisk together the margarine and 450g (1lb) of the sugar until light and fluffy. Add the vanilla essence and the eggs, one at a time, whisking after each addition.

3. In another bowl, combine the flour, the baking powder, bicarbonate of soda and salt. Then add to the egg mixture alternately with the yogurt, whisking just enough to keep the batter smooth.

4. In yet another bowl, mix the remaining sugar, pecans, berries and cinnamon.

5. Spoon enough batter into the tube tin to cover the base. Sprinkle evenly with half the fruit mixture. Add another layer of batter and the remainder of the fruit, then cover with the remaining batter. Smooth the top and tap the tin on the worktop to settle the contents.

6. Bake in the centre of the oven for 70 minutes, until a toothpick inserted into the cake comes out clean.

7. Remove from the oven and cool in the tin for 15 minutes, then carefully remove from the tin and continue cooling on a wire rack. Then ice the cake if you desire.

Chocolate and cherry brownies

Could anything possibly make a brownie better than it already is? Fruit? Try these and see if you agree with me. Last year I gave this recipe to a little 12-year-old friend and they turned out perfectly – not too sweet and nicely gooey.

Makes 24

You will need:
300g (11oz) unsalted butter
300g (11oz) 70% plain chocolate, roughly chopped
5 large eggs
450g (1lb) caster sugar
1 tbsp vanilla essence
200g (7oz) plain flour
1 tsp salt
250g (9oz) dried cherries

1. Preheat the oven to 180°C (350°F/Gas Mark 4). Line a 23 x 32.5cm (9 x 13in) baking tin with straight sides with parchment paper.

2. Place the butter and chocolate in a bowl over a saucepan of simmering water and melt, stirring occasionally,

being careful not to overheat to the point where the chocolate bubbles. Alternatively, melt in the microwave. Cool slightly.

3. In another bowl, whisk the eggs, sugar and the vanilla essence together until the mixture is thick and creamy and coats the back of a spoon. Whisk into the chocolate mixture.

4. Sift the flour with the salt, then add to the main mixture, continuing to whisk until smooth. Fold in the cherries.

5. Pour the batter into the baking tin, smoothing the top. Bake for 20–25 minutes, until there is a light brown crust, just starting to crack. It should not wobble, but will still be gooey on the inside. Cool for 20 minutes in the pan on a wire rack.

6. These brownies are easier to cut when they are cold, so if you are nervous (or prefer your chocolate fix cold), put the pan in the fridge for a little while, remove the parchment paper and cut into 24 pieces.

Old-fashioned lemonade

Traditional lemonade is *not* the fizzy drink we have come to know it as today – 'real' lemonade is made from freshly squeezed lemons, and is one of the greatest thirst-quenching drinks you can possibly have. It is perfect for those hot summer picnics.

Makes 2 litres (3 ½ pints)

> You will need:
> 450g (1lb) sugar
> 240ml (8fl oz) filtered water, plus extra for topping up
> 240ml (8fl oz) freshly squeezed lemon juice
> Ice

1. Combine the filtered water and sugar in a saucepan and heat, stirring, to dissolve the sugar and make a syrup.

2. Add the freshly squeezed lemon juice. Stir.

3. Add water to make up to 2 litres (3½ pints) of lemonade. Then drop in some ice and serve ice-cold.

Iced coffee

To my mind, in the summer good iced coffee is better than dessert! Somehow, instant coffee always tastes better than brewed for this drink and sugar substitute dissolves more easily. If you want to be really sinful, add a scoop of vanilla, coffee or chocolate ice cream to the finished drink.

Makes: 1 glassful

You will need:
Mugful of instant coffee, mixed the way you like it, and cooled
Sugar or sugar substitute to taste
Milk or cream
Ice cubes
Scoop of ice cream (optional)

1. Pour the coffee into a tall glass, add sugar or sugar substitute and stir to mix, then add the milk or cream.

2. Fill the glass with ice cubes, leaving a little space for your ice cream, if using, then add that as well.

3. When the coffee is so cold it almost makes your teeth hurt, insert a straw into the glass and sip.

Plants and Pets

Advice for the non-green-fingered

Whether you have inherited a mature garden, are starting from scratch, are lucky enough to have an allotment, or grow a few pot plants, you are in the majority if you have some interest in gardening. Most people do, either as a means of self-sustenance, growing vegetables or fruit, or because they like beautiful greenery and flowers. Here are some tips for the beginner gardener:

❀ Whatever the size of your garden, your commitment and knowledge should equal your space. Gardening can be a very expensive hobby and there is no point in taking it on if you are not going to devote to it the time it needs (unless you plan to hire a gardener).

�֎ Know one thing for certain. Gardening does not provide instant gratification. It's a bit like parenting – it needs patience and time. A good garden also needs planning. Read books and magazines to get tips and ideas, and visit public gardens and flower shows to familiarize yourself with unfamiliar plants.

✖ If you are a complete novice, enlist the help of someone who has the experience to teach you the rudiments. You'll learn more as you go along, most likely through trial and error. For instance, knowing what type of soil you have is important when deciding what you want to grow.

✖ When gardening indoors, if someone gives you a pot plant and it doesn't have any instructions on how to care for it, ask a florist, a nursery or a knowledgeable friend.

✖ Two of the most common causes of pot-plant death are overwatering and underwatering. If you follow the instructions that came with the plant, or follow advice from your local garden centre, you should be able to get watering right and your plants will thrive. If not, take heart. Even experienced gardeners sometimes make mistakes.

Growing your own food

There is nothing quite so satisfying as eating food you have grown yourself. If you have a garden or an allotment and want to grow vegetables and fruit, you will be rewarded with the freshest produce you can imagine. Here are some useful hints:

❀ When planting vegetables make sure you clear the soil of any stones, and mix in some compost to keep the soil nice and moist.

❀ If you are planting lettuces and salad leaves, pick the leaves regularly to encourage new growth and don't sow all your seeds at the same time unless you want to provide salad for all the neighbours.

❀ Slugs are a common scourge of vegetable patches, but you can see them off swiftly with a sprinkling of salt.

❀ Fruits are a little trickier to grow than vegetables, so choose those that suit the climate and the space you have available. Ask other gardeners what works for them.

Repotting plants

House plants need repotting occasionally, when they outgrow their pots or when the soil is depleted of nutrients. Repotting is a reasonably messy procedure, so you might want to do it outdoors if you have a choice; if not, cover the area you are working on with newspaper.

1. Don't make the mistake of repotting the plant into a very large pot when it is still small. This will *not* encourage growth, but will be too big a change for it. Choose a pot that is the next size up.

2. First of all, cover the drainage hole with a circle of outworn nylon tights, a bit of broken clay pot or a few stones, then add a compost appropriate for the type of plant.

3. Tease out the rootball a bit (that means working it out of the plant pot shape gently). Insert the rootball into the compost so that the top is at the same level as in the previous pot. Add more compost, if necessary, and press down firmly.

4. Give the plant a drink of water and set it where you'd like it, giving it a chance to acclimatize to its new environment.

Herbs

Growing your own herbs is extremely beneficial – not only will they make your food tasty, they also have natural healing properties (see page 47–8 for herbal remedies). Below are some useful suggestions before you start planting.

�֎ Some herbs prefer direct sunlight, while others prefer shade – make sure you know which are which to be sure they thrive. Chives, lavender, rosemary, thyme and sage are all sun lovers, while basil, parsley and rocket prefer enough shade to keep the soil nice and moist.

✤ Herbs are happiest when planted in soil outdoors, but if you don't have the space, you can always grow them in containers, window boxes, or hanging baskets. Do be aware, though, that they will require more care than herbs planted outside – so give them a good soil-based compost to grow in.

✤ Some herbs are annuals, some perennials. Basil, coriander, dill and borage are annual herbs; oregano, lavender, thyme, chives and rosemary are perennials. Annuals have to be planted from seed each year, while perennials can mostly be grown from small plants. If you live in a climate with cold winters, it is advisable to keep your perennial herbs either in a greenhouse or indoors until the spring returns.

Weeds

Weeds can be rather attractive. As long as they are not choking plants that I am trying to grow, they look as if they belong in the garden. So my philosophy is: don't try to eradicate weeds completely. Just deal with them often, a little at a time.

You don't even have to use weedkiller. If you weed often, you can just pull them out by hand. If you don't know the difference between a weed and a cultivated plant, tug on it. If it comes out of the ground easily, it's not a weed – or so the old gardening joke goes! Of course, the best solution is to get to know enough about plants so that you can recognize the difference.

Annual weeds can be put in the compost bin. Perennial weeds – the ones that show their heads year after year – need to be put in the rubbish, because even the smallest bit of root will allow it to grow just to annoy you next year.

Choosing an appropriate family pet

Sometimes deciding on a new pet is easy – you or your family has had this particular type of animal before, or you visit a pet shop or rescue centre and fall in love. Sometimes it's not so easy.

You have to feel comfortable with the pet you choose, cat, dog, bird, reptile or anything else. Your child may promise to feed it, walk it, clean up after it, but somehow, you will probably end up doing most of the work. You have to be prepared to care for it in sickness and in health. Otherwise, no matter how much your children plead with you, don't do it!

Things to bear in mind when choosing a family pet are:

- how easy the animal will be to housetrain – sometimes buying older animals that are already house-trained, rather than say a kitten or a puppy that you will have to train yourself, is easiest when you have children to consider.

- whether there's a risk of allergies – make sure your children aren't allergic to fur before buying your pet. It will be hard for both your children and the animal if you have to take it back after a brief time because it's making them ill.

- how much time you have to devote to the animal. Dogs need regular walking; cats are far more independent; fish are a busy parent/grandparent's dream!

✵ whatever animal you choose, the key to having a true 'family' pet – one that is gentle, loyal and loving – is to treat the animal as a beloved family member and to provide the training and care it deserves. It's not enough to get a pet 'for the kids'. A pet is not a temporary playmate for children, but will be a family member for years, and is dependent on you and your family for its wellbeing.

Involving your children in pet maintenance

Allowing your child to help care for a pet will teach them responsibility and instil a feeling of accomplishment. You should choose chores that are appropriate for the age of your child. Even very young children can be involved in some way, for example, choosing a new toy, or putting the food bowl down.

The best way to teach your children how to act towards pets is to be a good example to them.

✵ You must make certain that your children don't pull the animal's tail or ears; that they never tease, strike or chase the pet; and that they never put their fingers into the animal's mouth.

✵ Teach your children how to pick up the animal and how to stroke it without upsetting it, and ensure your children wash their hands after handling the pet.

- You should involve your children in training, which will not only make your animal better-mannered, but will teach your children humane treatment and effective communication. It will also make your life easier.

- If you have a pet that needs regular exercise, you must understand that this is something that you have to do day in and day out, regardless of the weather or how busy you are. Remember, too, that if your dog needs to relieve itself, it can only cross its legs for so long before it has an accident.

Puppy behaviour and training

The first week or so that you have a new puppy or dog is critical to its training. First of all, the entire family should agree on its routine, and what the rules and responsibilities are. If the agreement was that the puppy sleeps in a crate, changing your mind and taking it into your bed will just cause trouble.

It's true that a new puppy has been taken away from its mother, sisters and brothers and will feel vulnerable. What it needs is security and routine. Cover the floor of its 'bedroom' with newspapers and put food and water bowls in one corner of the room. Scatter appropriate soft toys. When playing with the new arrival, do so quietly and gently and, if it looks as if the puppy wants to sleep, let it. Puppies, like human babies, need lots of sleep.

If this is your first puppy, ask for advice from the owner or rescue centre or someone you respect who has a well-mannered pet. Also, think seriously about professional dog-training courses unless you are very certain you can do it yourself.

If you have small children, it is probably safer to have an adult dog that has not been abused in any way. A well-treated, happy, calm dog will offer you and your children love and loyalty. If it's possible, find out about the dog's routine and feeding habits from the previous owner.

Cleaning up after pets

All pets need cleaning up after, and some more than others. Here are some basic tips for common family pets:

- Fish tank maintenance – opinion varies about how frequently you should change the water of your fish tank, but since it seems generally accepted that a complete water change gives fish a bit of a nasty shock to their system, it is advisable that you change up to 20 per cent of the water once every two to three weeks.

- Bathing and brushing furry pets regularly will minimize the amount of hair they shed around the house.

- If you do have to clean up fur in the house use a lint roller – they are usually small enough to pop into your bag if have to get rid of dog hair in the car.

- Litter train kittens and puppies as soon as possible – the sooner they learn to use the litter tray the sooner you will have peace of mind that your carpets and furniture won't be soiled.

- If you have a dog, always go on dog walks equipped with plastic bags to clear up any mess it makes along the way.

Protecting your furniture from pets

If you have cats or dogs, it is almost inevitable that your furniture will be at risk of scratches – particularly from cats. It is natural for cats, as predatory animals, to sharpen their claws, so you won't be able to stop their instinctive urge to do so. The best method is to provide them with a scratching post, since this will divert them away from your furniture.

If you can bear the smell, bitter orange or bitter apple spray acts as a deterrent for cats, so giving your sofas and chairs a quick spray might do the trick.

Pets that provide food

We've all heard stories about the farm child about to tuck into a Sunday lunch of roast pork who says to his or her parents, 'Is that Rosie?' 'What a gruesome question!' you may think. But to farm children, this is just a fact of life. These animals may be seen as semi-pets but for farmers they are also a source of income and, at some point, may provide food for the family too.

It is the same with ducks, hens and geese. They may all have names, and in many cases provide eggs for their owners, but when they can no longer supply this food, they may become dinner themselves.

If this is the situation in your home, it is best to prepare your children by treating it as a natural and normal occurrence.

When your pet dies

The loss of a pet may be a child's first experience with death. The child may blame themself, their parents or the vet for not saving the pet. They may also feel guilty and depressed, and frightened that others they love may be taken from them.

Trying to protect your child by saying the pet ran away could cause your child to expect the pet's return – and feel betrayed after discovering the truth. Expressing your own grief may reassure your child that sadness is all right and help your child work through their feelings.

Advice about Children

Talking and listening

At times, all adults are guilty of telling children to 'hurry up' and 'do it quickly', or of saying 'don't talk to me now, I'm busy'. Sometimes this is justified, but most often, it is out of habit. If you can't talk to the child at that moment because you truly are busy, tell them, 'I'm sorry, but I'm in the middle of X right now. Can we talk about it when I've finished? I won't be long.'

Children get bored. They seem to get even more bored when you are talking to someone on the telephone, when you are adding up a column of numbers, when you are measuring out ingredients for a recipe – anything you might be doing instead of paying attention to them. So they interrupt you and you get irritated and say, 'Can't you see I'm busy?'

Aside from them telling you that the house is burning down

or something of equal consequence, you don't have to pander to the child's need to talk to you that minute. On the other hand, you don't want your child to think that you can't give him or her your attention at all. So when you find yourself in this situation, you have to offer an alternative time or place to talk. When you do eventually talk, sit down and really listen to what he or she has to say.

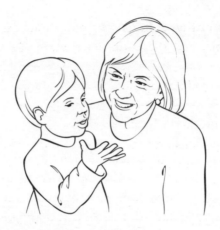

Don't always say no

Once, a long time ago, when I had little children, an older woman I knew told me I should be careful not to automatically say 'no' to my children. She said unless their requests were against my principles, unsafe or just plain wrong, I should say 'yes' to my children because it would make them happy and there would be a lot of instances where I would *have* to say 'no'. It was good advice and I pass it on. This doesn't, of course, mean spoiling the child – which it is terribly easy to do with children!

Discipline

'Spare the rod and spoil the child' is one of those sayings that has a very long history – some say harking back as far as the Book of Proverbs. Its meaning, then as now, is that if you love your children, you will chastise them for wrongdoing.

The idea of hitting children as a punishment is now deeply unacceptable, and there are much more effective ways of disciplining your child – and in a manner appropriate to their age. A toddler or pre-schooler could be taught about the 'naughty step'. One minute on the step for each year under five seems to be an acceptable length of time. Five minutes is sufficient for the next age group. If the child leaves the step, you must return them to it firmly and calmly.

Older children might benefit from having things taken away when their behaviour is inappropriate – mobile phones, video games, TVs, MP3s, CD and DVD players. They won't be at all happy, but it might teach them there are consequences to their actions.

Embarrassing your children/ grandchildren

No matter how you try to avoid it, at some point in your life you are going to embarrass your children or grandchildren; maybe many times.

Very young children tend to be adoring and unquestioning, but as they grow older and they become more aware of what other people may or may not be thinking they start to find the behaviour of the adults around them mortifying. Don't take it personally! There's a reason teenagers are stereotyped as sulking and disapproving of their parents. It's a phase, and it will pass. Soon they'll be adults and in no time at all they'll be embarrassing *their* children.

Little children, little problems

You never stop being a parent, whatever age your children are, but – as my mother used to say – 'little children, little problems; big children, big problems'.

Small children have problems that are usually easily solved, but as they get older, the problems get more complex and it is not usually possible to kiss them away. And when they start their own families, not only do they continue to call on your support but you also have the burden of grandchildren and *their* problems, sometimes in addition to those of your own elderly parents.

I always envisaged a future in which my children would go out on their own and there would be a window of normality before I had to worry about my parents. This didn't happen and, after talking to other people with families, I realize that it rarely does. But with all the problems come generations' worth of advice and support shared.

Solidarity

My children have never been very successful in pitting one parent against the other because we have always (at least publicly) put up a solid front. That's not to say they haven't tried. They have. Often. But they have never won. Whether they are a couple or living apart, parents should always sing from the same hymn book. And so should grandparents!

Times change

When my daughters were young and I was unable to collect them from school for some reason, there were a series of friends I could call on to do it for me. I, of course, returned the favour when they couldn't collect. No one at the school ever asked any questions or needed my prior permission to give my girls over to people who were, to them, perfect strangers. When I had to pick up my granddaughter, on the other hand, I practically had to prove that I wasn't a kidnapper – or worse.

There will be times when you cannot personally collect your child from school or an activity, so you should make a backup plan and arrange for a friend or family member to cover for you. And always alert the school to your arrangements to avoid confusion.

Showing favouritism

There are people who maintain that they love all their children or grandchildren 'the same'. However, in truth, while we love our children the same amount, we often love them in very different ways.

But loving them in different ways does not mean showing blatant favouritism to one child over another. When a child feels that, no matter what he does, it isn't good enough, he'll just stop trying.

You have to learn to know your children and sense when they are doing their personal best – if that truly is the case, it doesn't matter whether this is more or less than their siblings. Praise them when they have done well and disapprove when they haven't made an effort. Don't judge their achievements by comparing them with someone else. Life isn't a competition.

Anger management

Everyone gets angry. How it manifests itself, though, depends on a person's character and the situation.

What one should strive not to do is shout. Shouting at a child serves no purpose at all. It just upsets them. I have a very short fuse, so I have done my share of shouting, but have found that some other methods work far better.

If a child goes beyond the boundaries you have set for him/her or does something very naughty, it is wiser to say 'I'm too angry to discuss this right now' followed by 'give me a few minutes' or something similar rather than to lose your temper. But if you are going to say that, you must follow it up. And if it is your child who is angry or frustrated with you, try to calm him/her down before talking through the situation.

Biting your tongue and swallowing your anger, and never bringing up the matter again, will just lead children to assume they have got away with it, so it's best to discuss the situation when you are both calmer.

Competing to win

It has become the norm for schools and other organizations to shy away from presenting prizes for sporting achievements and the like, but there's nothing like a rush of adrenalin to tell you that you have done well, and also give you the incentive to do even better.

If children are taught that their best, and striving to improve their best, is a great accomplishment in itself, then they can cherish their achievements as much as the winners can their victory.

Good manners

A well-mannered child is not only a reflection of his or her parents, but is also better equipped to deal with life. When you teach your children manners, you are teaching them some lifelong survival skills. The old adage 'do unto others' applies here. If you want your children to treat others with respect, for instance, you must teach them this by respecting them. Children learn by example.

Most parents swear there are some things they will never say or do to their children, but generation after generation continues to do so. For example, you tell your child to do something and the response is 'Why?' This is usually answered with 'Because I said so.' What kind of an answer is that? An easy one, since you don't have to explain yourself. This only makes sense to a very small child who wouldn't understand your explanation. All others deserve one.

> ✿ 'Please', 'thank you', 'excuse me' and 'sorry' are
> still very much needed in everyone's vocabulary.
> It doesn't take very much time to add these words,
> but they make the world a much nicer place.

- 'Could you please not make so much noise' or 'Could we have a bit more quiet in here?' sounds much nicer than 'Stop that racket this instant' and is more likely to produce results. 'Could I please have...' will also go down better than 'I want...'

- By the same token, 'Excuse me' or 'Sorry' is far less aggressive than 'Move'.

- If you are going to apologize, you should *mean* you are sorry, rather than just playing lip service to the words.

- If someone says or does something hurtful to you, it is better to bite your tongue or count to ten rather than to lash back at them. There are some circumstances, though, where you have to say something – and, believe me, saying it the right way is an art that is learned through experience.

- It's a good idea to teach children a polite telephone manner. Answering the phone with your name is a good habit you can pass on to your children.

Thank yous

I was taught that if someone gave me a present, I had to write a note to thank them. I taught my children the same.

Although times have changed, good manners have not. It isn't acceptable to thank someone in a text or by email. Taking the time to write a note, or a postcard, to acknowledge the gift shows proper gratitude and appreciation of the thought that they put into choosing the present for you.

Such rudeness (for that's what it is) as not replying at all can result in that person not ever sending you a present again. After all, if it means so little to you, why should they?

Giving and getting presents

There's nothing that compares with getting a present that has been made for you by someone you love. It isn't about how much the gift costs. The best ones are pictures children have drawn for you, cards they have made, rocks they have painted and pottery, misshapen or beautifully crafted. It's a cliché but a gift given from the heart means so much more than anything most money can buy.

Bedtime

Children do need a bedtime routine, but it can be tricky to find one that works. Not only will it vary from family to family, but you may find what works for one of your children is completely different from what works for another. But it *is* important to find a settled routine to ensure they get proper rest.

Aiming for certain times to get children fed, washed and ready for bed is most definitely a wise idea, but do not get distressed if this doesn't always go according to plan. One tactic that can work is to get your toddler to put favourite toys to bed before jumping in him- or herself.

Time will help you and your child settle into a routine that works for you, and of course the older they get the more able they are to get themselves ready for bed at a respectable hour. I must say I was very pleased when, as a teenager, one of my girls got up from the sofa at a perfectly decent hour and announced, 'It's my bedtime. Goodnight all.'

Safety precautions

Keeping your child safe is your number one priority as a parent, but as careful as you are to keep your children out of harm's way, they will find a way to hurt themselves and the best you can do is try to anticipate problems and prevent them. Should the unthinkable happen, whether your child incurs a physical or emotional injury, deal with the situation as calmly as you can – it will help them realize that it isn't the end of the world and that it will pass.

How to get your child to eat

Try to introduce your child to a great variety of different foods as early as possible. I remember my first daughter gumming a steak before she had the teeth to chew it. I also remember my girls loving the foreign dishes I cooked – quite fiery Indian curries and very oddly seasoned (for a young palate) Chinese fare.

If you have cooked a certain ingredient a particular way and your child has not been impressed, cook it a different way next time. Some children don't like pasta, rice, chicken with bones, any fish at all, anything green, juice with 'bits' in it, any sort of fruit… Basically, they are fussy eaters. But the worst thing you can do is make the dinner table a battleground. If a child says they don't like something even before it hits their fork, ask them to taste it – to take a 'brownie bite'. They may be surprised, or the reality may not be to their taste. 'Never mind,' you can tell them, 'just leave it.'

There will invariably be other things on their plate that they find more palatable.

Do not expect children always to like the same foods. 'But you *loved* that last week,' makes no difference, and neither should you expect logic in food thinking. Just because a child likes tomatoes has no bearing whatsoever on whether they will like tomato sauce or even tomatoes in their salad.

Finally, do not expect all your children to have the same food tastes. However, never fall into the trap that one beleaguered lady I know fell into. When her adult children come to her for Sunday lunch, she prepares at least three different potato dishes because one wants mash, one wants roasties… Another woman roasts chicken, beef and pork for her lot to choose from. If this is your situation and you want to keep all of your children happy, you must allow some of them to be somewhat *un*happy some of the time or you will wear yourself out.

Telling the truth and bending it

I think it's fair to say that all of us want our children to be truthful. And yet, if we're truthful, all of us lie sometimes, or if not lie, omit. Why do children lie? For the same reason as adults – it is usually a means to avoid blame or punishment, or with older children, to skirt topics that are difficult or embarrassing. Sometimes they lie so that their parents won't be disappointed in them. I have read that the more intelligent the child, the younger and better the liar. Parents lie too –

about their feelings, their motives, all sorts of things. And it is we who teach our children to tell untruths, both directly and tacitly. Sometimes we wish they *would* lie when they tell our secrets!

There isn't any way we can prevent our children from lying. But we can try to teach them (and ourselves) the difference between a white lie, told to spare someone's feelings, and the lie that is told for no good reason.

N.B. Don't ever lie to your children about a procedure not hurting – an injection or stitches, for instance, or tell them you are going somewhere nice when you are trundling them off to the doctor or dentist. They will never trust you again.

Perception

It's true that you can't tell a book by its cover. People are not always as they are perceived to be by their appearance. All blondes are not dumb, all redheads are not quick-tempered and your accent is not a good barometer of your intelligence. Children aren't born with these preconceived ideas – they are taught them by the society around them.

Bullying

Bullying has no doubt always prevailed, but I have never had any first-hand personal experience of it.

In my eldest granddaughter's primary school in London, they had a bully-busting campaign and my granddaughter was chosen as one of the pupil bully-busters. As I understand it, the children who were chosen were identified to the other pupils so that if anyone had a problem, they could go and talk to one of their peers instead of 'ratting' on another child to their teacher.

The scheme apparently worked well and the children were rewarded when one day the Queen came to the school to meet the chosen bully-busters. She walked up to my granddaughter and said, 'How kind of you to give up your playtime to help other children.' My granddaughter is usually quite a chatterbox, but she was briefly struck inarticulate and replied, 'It's all right!' Despite her speechlessness, I know that helping other children to combat bullying taught her and the other children valuable lessons, as well as giving victims a non-intimidating forum to reveal what they were going through. I hope the scheme is implemented in more schools.

Familes and Daily Life

Personal relationships

Families can be the greatest source of support and strength, but they can also cause no end of headaches! This section offers some simple advice to help you navigate you through the tricky times.

New babies/sibling rivalry

Often a child will respond to a new baby with joy and curiosity, but sometimes perfectly natural feelings of jealousy can kick in and make a sibling resent the newcomer. Try to involve the older child in the baby's arrival, and make him/her feel very much a part of this exciting event.

As your children grow older, particularly as they enter their teenage years, siblings may well rub each other up the wrong way. All families are different, but it is often wisest to let your children sort out their differences between themselves, providing that they are not actually hurting each other. Very often their disputes will be short-lived, and allowing them to play it out between themselves rather than separating them and making them bottle up their anger can be beneficial.

Dealing with divorce

Divorce is traumatic enough when there are only two of you. When there are children involved, it is even harder.

Divorce can lead to feelings of anger towards one or both of the parents, and the child/children may conclude that in some way the split is their fault. They may be forced by circumstances to live in a different place from the family home and, sometimes, even in a different city or country.

In an ideal world, the parents will still speak to each other and both of them will have access to the children. In the real world, there is often resentment. It is absolutely imperative, however, that the children are your number one priority in these situations – and that you reassure them that while mummy and daddy are no longer together it is *not* their fault and that they are as loved as ever by both of you. Arguing in front of the children will only add to their feelings of confusion and hurt, so make sure you restrict any disagreements to a space well out of hearing range of your offspring.

Being a grandparent

Parenting isn't easy because no one can tell you how to be a good one. What makes a good grandparent is just as elusive. The person you are will dictate your approach to your grandchildren, but here are a few simple tips to bear in mind.

- When you're babysitting, make sure you get all the information you can from the parents about what the child should and shouldn't do – e.g. nap times, allergies, emergency numbers etc.

- Remember that at the end of the day (or weekend or week) you will hand the children back to their parents, so try as far as possible to keep to the same rules as they do to prevent the child from becoming confused.

Grandchildren and grandparents often have a special bond, with the same unconditional love that a parent feels – and it is precisely this unconditional love that makes a great grandparent, and what makes being a grandparent so great.

Family get-togethers

Holidays and travel

Far from being blissful and laid-back, holidays can sometimes be very stressful, especially when you are visiting family or taking your family somewhere unfamiliar. I am in awe of those families with tiny children who endure endless hours in airports and aeroplanes to go on holiday. If they are visiting family, parents or grandparents, I can understand it, but otherwise it just seems like a nightmare to me. Taking little children to another country to see the sights might sound like a good idea, but they would be just as happy sitting on a beach with a bucket and spade. They probably won't even remember the trip when they get older.

If you are doing it for yourselves rather than the children, that's fine, but maybe in that case, you would be better off going without them if you have a suitable babysitter.

Christmas

I have titled this 'Christmas', but you can apply it to any religious, family or national holiday you like. In the 'good old days', none of the decorations or festivities started three months early. Stretching an occasion to this point does seem to cause the meaning of it to become lost, but the idea of a family Christmas shouldn't be lost in commercialization. Of course, the reality of spending a couple of days – or a couple of weeks – with your family all together does not always make for a relaxing holiday, and for some people it is better for all concerned that they do not gather in this way. It is quite common these days for groups of friends to get together to celebrate these occasions.

Birthdays

Birthdays can be joyous occasions, particularly for children, but not everyone enjoys celebrating them, and some people in fact find them rather stressful times. We can generally accept that people are all very different from each other but find it baffling when we don't all respond to things with a 'typical' response. If a member of your family or a friend doesn't enjoy celebrating their birthday with a big bash, find out what that person would prefer to do – if anything at all.

Weddings and funerals

Nothing brings family and friends together as much as weddings and funerals. A wedding is a happy occasion and a funeral is a sad one, but it isn't always all one or the other.

Some girls plan their weddings from the age of five and it is often the woman's vision that drives what kind of wedding a couple has. It is important not to forget that while you might have found the perfect man to fit into your dream wedding, his own dream wedding might not exactly match yours – so try to incorporate both sets of ideas and hopes so it is a perfect day for the two of you, not just the one.

Funerals are always extremely difficult and upsetting occasions. It has become increasingly popular, however, to make the focus of the funeral a celebration of the dead person's life, to enable those gathered to remember all the best things about the person they have loved. It seems a fitting and respectful way to pay tribute to someone's life, rather than to simply mourn their death.

Remembering to make memories

Photographs

Often the firstborn is photographed ad nauseam – hundreds of photographs are taken at every stage of the baby's development (digital cameras have exacerbated this). Then the next child comes along and the urge isn't so great. But in years to come you will regret it if you don't keep a photographic record of all your children's lives, so make photo albums for each child. It's not only a great way to remember those early precious days for you, but for your children it is a wonderful window into a time that they themselves will be highly unlikely to remember.

Baby books

The same applies to baby books – include weight, height and other statistics, the lock of hair after the first haircut and a bunch of other trivia, such as the date of their first tooth.

It may not seem important to register all of this in print at the time it happens, but twenty or thirty or forty years on, you will wish you had.

Correspondence

Then there are the letters and postcards that your children wrote when they were on a school trip or away at summer camp. You probably didn't keep any of them. I wish I'd kept the one my eldest wrote from girl-scout camp that was supposed to make me feel guilty. It said: 'I HATE this place. All the girls are horrible to me. The food is foul and the tents leak. Take me away from here immediately!' Two days later I got a completely differently toned postcard, telling me about all the wonderful activities and how nice all her new friends were. It was a very angst-ridden forty-eight hours.

Written correspondence from your children – at whatever age – provides wonderful keepsakes for the family, and is often a great source of entertainment, and even comfort.

Children's drawings and gifts

Children like to draw and make things. My grandchildren have made us lots of gifts, which we cherish. We have drawings, painted rocks, collages made from photos and greetings cards, pottery and brass rubbings – all proudly displayed. Encourage children to be crafty with their hands, and get stuck in with them! It will inspire their creativity, and you will be left with wonderful memories of these moments that you have shared together.

Finding your roots

My mother was the youngest of nine children and I had loads of cousins whom I hadn't seen since I was a child, so I set out to meet them, or at least to establish email contact with those who were so inclined. I'm really glad I did. It continues to be very heart-warming to have lots of family.

Genealogy has understandably become very popular, as it teaches you so much about who you are and where you and your family have come from – and, as I did, you might discover new family members you never knew existed.

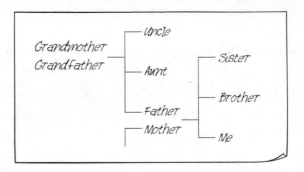

Grudges

Don't hold grudges. There will always be things people have done that have hurt or angered you, but by holding on to that injury you only hurt yourself – not the person who hurt you.

Balancing the budget

It seems a rather tiresome thing to do but keeping a notebook with a record of your incoming and outgoing money really is one of the wisest things you can do. While it may seem unnecessarily detailed to keep a daily note of what you're spending, in the long run it will give you control over your money – it is so easy with bank cards to pay for things and instantly forget what you have paid out. With a written record of your spending habits you will soon spot ways in which you can save money when you see what your money is being spent on.

Neither a borrower nor a lender be

It is an old saying but there is a good reason it has stood the test of time – because it is extremely sage advice.

Credit cards have encouraged a society where spending money we don't have is deemed perfectly acceptable, but it is a dangerous habit to get into. If you do have a credit card, try to limit yourself on the number of transactions that you put on it over the course of a year – and to avoid paying climbing interest rates, pay it off as quickly as you possibly can.

Equally, while we all like to help out a friend in need, lending money can lead to trouble – if the person is late paying you back, or indeed is completely unable to return the money, it can put a great strain on even the closest of friendships. If you do find yourself in a position where you are lending money to a friend, make sure you are both clear on the terms of the loan, and agree a manageable date by which all the money must be paid back.

Money saving tips

When times get tough financially, it can be hard to know where to begin in trying to sort things out. If the larger outgoings are unavoidable, or too much to contemplate saving initially, start looking at the small areas where you can save your pennies (and thereby also your pounds). Here are a few suggestions:

- Get your books and DVDs from the library – it's very rare that you will read the same book or watch the same film within a year of reading or seeing it the first time, so why not save an awful lot of money and rent them from your local library? Not only will you be benefitting your purse but you'll be supporting your local community at the same time.

- Switch off all lights when you're not in the room, likewise heaters and fires. And make sure your taps and your shower aren't dripping away your money!

- Make a family (and friends if possible) pact to limit the amount of money you spend on gift giving. Not only does this help you all out financially, it can inspire more creative and thoughtful present buying.

- Prepare your own food rather than buying ready-made meals – it is so much cheaper to whip up your own meals. And the health benefits are huge, too, since ready-made meals will almost always have far more salt and fat in them than anything you will make yourself.

The value of lists

I confess! I am an inveterate listomaniac. I make shopping lists, birthday and anniversary lists, appointment lists, to-do lists and several others. Either I am an obsessive-compulsive person or very organized; I'm not sure which. Maybe both. Here is why I do it.

Shopping lists

There is no way I am going to remember everything I've run out of that needs replacing, so I keep a running list in my kitchen of fresh produce, groceries, household cleaners, health and hygiene items. I keep them all on one list. Items that get replaced when I walk to the shops up the road get erased; the others remain on the list until the next supermarket shop. It saves me having to run around the house looking to see what I need just prior to going shopping.

Birthday lists

Everyone is amazed that we always remember birthdays and anniversaries. It's very simple: when someone mentions a date, you record it on your computer or mobile calendar. So much easier than the filofax used to be!

Addresses and telephone numbers

I accidentally fried both my mobile and my SIM card a little while ago, and it took me ages to key in all the telephone numbers I had in my phone. Luckily, most of them were on my computer and what I didn't have, my husband did. It's a good idea to keep two printed copies of all your contacts – that way if technology fails you, or if you lose one set, you won't lose your friendships too!

Appointments

It's easy to forget or mis-remember the date of an appointment, so make a note in your diary. We were invited for drinks at a neighbour's with another couple. But we were accidentally invited on separate days because the hostess couldn't find her diary when she asked our other friends. If I hadn't spoken to the other couple, the poor lady would have had to entertain on two evenings instead of one.

To-do lists

This may sound simplistic, but the only way to organize your day, week or life is to have a clear idea of what you need or want to do. You can either do this mentally by making a list in your head, or manually by writing it down. I prefer to write it so that I can prioritize. This does not mean that I never get diverted, but it's less likely if I have some idea of what I have to cover and how much time to allocate.

Fashion

Don't panic

Never buy clothes when you are in a panic. The chances are you will go for something you may never wear again. If it's a special occasion, you probably already have an outfit in your wardrobe that is perfect. Don't worry if you have worn it before with the same people. They won't remember and even if they do, who cares? If it fits well and is flattering, you should feel good about it.

Updating your wardrobe

Even if you detest shopping, everyone likes something new once in a while. If you are a clever shopper, you can upgrade your wardrobe without having to replace it every year. Here are some handy tips:

- ❀ Don't buy into too many new trends. The tulip skirt you crave this year will probably go the way the puffball went in the 1980s. Fashion designers come up with new silhouettes every season so that customers will buy new things.

- ❀ Stick to more classic shapes in good fabrics with quality workmanship and you will always look fine and certainly get your money's worth. If you start getting tired of a jacket, you can always replace the buttons for a new look.

⌘ Other update options include adding some lovely lace or brocade, threading a ribbon through a sweater or changing the way you wear something, such as belting a jacket, using a long beaded necklace as a belt for trousers or re-thinking which separates go together.

Charity shops

Charity shops, especially those in affluent areas, are wonderful places to buy clothes. The fact is that people get bored with their clothes, they lose and gain weight, and sometimes someone dies and the family needs to clear out the wardrobe. Their loss or gain or boredom can provide you with a bargain if you put in the time to look.

Looking after your clothes

There's no point in buying a beautiful frock and after you've worn it, stepping out of it and leaving it in a crumpled heap on the floor. That's the way to disaster. When you undress at the end of the day, examine your clothing for stains and small tears and if you find any, either deal with them there and then or – and probably more practically – fold the item and place it where you can deal with the problem later. Make sure you wash, dry clean or make any necessary repairs as soon as possible.

If buttons are loose, they will get lost, so either pin or tape them to the article of clothing. A handy tip for preventing buttons falling off is to brush some clear nail varnish onto the thread that holds the button in place. When it dries it will have fortified the thread – and hopefully the button should stay in place for as long as your garment lasts!

Even if your clothes are clean, you should wash or dry-clean them at the end of the season's wear before you fold them away for the next year to discourage moths and other insects. Ironing the clothes you are putting away is a waste of time – better to do that when you bring them out again.

Putting yourself together

Some people can do it naturally, others need a bit of help – but no matter what your fashion budget is, you can make the best of your appearance.

I get very cross when I read what people 'should' be wearing at various ages. Forget 'mutton dressed as lamb' and take a good, hard look at yourself in the mirror. Obviously you don't want to look like a teenager if you are a grandmother even if you have a teenage shape, but you don't have to look like *your* grandmother, either. The older you are, the more you will find that coverage can be your friend; bare legs, low-cut tops and sleeveless dresses are probably best avoided. But if trusted friends/family/partners say you can still carry it off with grace, then sometimes you can break the rules.

You should dress to accentuate your good points. Everyone has some good points even though we think we're too fat, too thin, too tall, too short and so on. If you are confused about what will make you look more attractive, there are many articles in books and magazines about how to dress for your body shape. You can also enlist the help of a good friend, your mother, your sisters or even your daughters (but only if you think they have a sense of style).

Make-up and beauty tips

One of the greatest joys in life can be learning make-up tips from your mother or grandmother. Watching them do their daily application is the very first make-up lesson most girls will get. Here are a few tips that you can pass onto the next generation:

A good base

No, not foundation – the best base is healthy, glowing skin. To make sure you have the best possible canvas to work on, ensure you drink plenty of water, that you eat plenty of fruit and vegetables, and that you get a good daily dosage of fresh air.

Before and after

It is essential that before applying make-up your skin is clean and properly moisturised, or your make-up will not go on evenly. And it is even more important that you wash your skin thoroughly at night to remove every last trace of make-up, to prevent your pores clogging up and creating spots, or if you leave eye make-up on, the risk of infections.

The either/or rule

Make-up is supposed to enhance, rather than disguise your features, so stick to this timeless rule – either accentuate your eyes or your lips, not both at once. So, if you're wearing strong eye make-up, keep your lip colour neutral, and if you choose a bright lip shade, keep your eyes natural.

Preserving your make-up

Surprisingly, the fridge can be your best friend when it comes to preserving and lengthening the life of your make-up. Lipsticks and nail varnishes will all last considerably longer if you keep them in your refrigerator. However, it's advisable to keep them in a sealed plastic container or bag to ensure they do not come into contact with any food.

Some make-up, however, should be replaced regularly. To avoid eye infections, mascara and liquid eyeliner should be replaced every three months. Foundation mixtures can become uneven over time, so should be replaced every six months or so.

Finding your signature scent

Choosing a perfume is a highly individual experience. Not only are we all attracted to very different smells, but one scent can smell very different on two separate people due to the chemical reaction of the perfume on skin. Also, a scent that you fall in love with as a teenager you might find completely repellent as an adult. Go to your local cosmetics shop or the perfume section of your local department store and spend plenty of time sniffing each scent before you make your decision. Most stores provide sticks on which to spray the perfume, to prevent you having to douse yourself in countless different scents.

Natural beauty

If you prefer to use natural products to enhance your looks, there are plenty of options – you just have to look in your kitchen for ingredients!

- Herbs to help remove dandruff include witchhazel bark, sage and rosemary.

- To keep your body beautiful, indulge in a herbal bath – to soothe dry, itchy skin you should include a cupful of equal quantities of comfrey oil and extract of lady's mantle; for a soothing bath at the end of the day use a mixture of extract of chamomile, valerian and cowslips.

- For clearer, spot-free skin, have a good morning and evening wash with witch hazel, which you can buy at your local pharmacy.

HERBAL SHAMPOO

If you want to try to make your own herbal shampoo, here's a mixture with suggested herbs for different hair colours.

> You will need:
> 30g (1oz) of herbs (chamomile for blondes; ginger or red hibiscus for redheads; sage or raspberry leaves for brunettes)
> ½oz (15g) nettles (which contains nutrients to encourage hair growth)
> 300ml (½ pint of water)
> 30g (1oz) of castile soap, grated
> Empty 300ml (½ pint) bottle or container

Bring the water to the boil, then add the herbs and nettles and stir. Take the pan off the boil, and ideally leave to stand overnight (or if you are pushed for time, leave for as many hours as you possibly can). In the morning, strain off the herbs pour the remaining water back into your saucepan and put it on a gentle heat on the hob. Stir in the grated castile soap until it has all melted into the mixture. Then take the pan off the heat and allow the mixture to cool before pouring it into your bottle. The shampoo is now ready to be used. Be aware that this should not be kept for much longer than six to eight weeks.

Making your own gifts

I find gifts that are made, rather than bought, much more thoughtful. There are many ways in which you can use your skills to make the perfect present for someone special. The only caveat is time.

Knitting and sewing

If you are handy with a needle, you can make someone's day with a beautiful one-off piece of clothing, or a toy for a child, or creative accessories for children and adults alike.

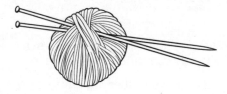

CLOTHES

If you know the person's size and tastes, you can stitch together an item of clothing, but beware of the handmade-looking sweater! The curse of many a Christmas morning... Most haberdashery sections of department stores will stock knitting patterns, and you can get a wide range online.

TOYS

Obviously, you must bear in mind the age of the child you are making the toy for, from a safety point of view as much as anything – you don't want a month-old child stuffing a woollen toy in its mouth. Classic toys, such as teddy bears and dolls, *never* go out of fashion, and should hopefully stay firm favourites long after the latest 'It' toy has disappeared from the shelves. Again, patterns for toys can be found online and in knitting magazines.

ACCESSORIES

If winter is on its way, a safe bet for a homemade gift is a good thick woollen scarf, hat or gloves. But if you're really handy with a needle and thread, knitting needles, or indeed any kind of crafts, you can come up with all sorts of goodies – handbags, purses, blankets, throws, jewellery and so on.

Here's a quick make-it-yourself gift that is perfect for girls of all ages – a floral hair accessory.

> You will need:
> Needle and thread
> A fabric flower (available from haberdashers and online)
> Either a plain hairclip or hairband
> Optional extras: glitter, ribbons, sequins etc.

This is such an easy thing to make but is a beautiful present to receive. You simply have to cut the stem of your fabric flower and then, taking your needle and a good strong thread, sew it onto the hairclip or hairband with a few stitches to secure it tightly. Then all you need to do is add any other decorations you want – perhaps you could stitch on a couple of ribbons to flow from the flower, or you could add sequins or glitter to give it extra dazzle. Make sure you wrap it beautifully!

Cooking and baking

Since cooking and baking are pretty time-intensive, if you are making large batches, consider where you are going to store all these treats until you can wrap and distribute them. If your fridge does not have enough space, you will have to prepare food that can be put into airtight containers and stored at room temperature. Here are some perfect foodie gifts that will delight children and adults alike:

CUPCAKES

Baking cupcakes with your grandchildren can be a satisfying and creative activity – and the result is the perfect-sized cake for little fingers.

Makes 18

You will need:
225g (8oz) plain flour
275g (10oz) caster sugar
1 tbsp baking powder
½ tsp salt
110g (4oz) solid vegetable fat or butter
240ml (8fl oz) milk
1 tsp vanilla essence
2 large eggs, beaten

1. Preheat the oven to 180°C (350°F/Gas Mark 4). Line fairy-cake or muffin tins with paper liners.

2. In a large bowl, mix together the flour, sugar, baking powder and salt. Add the fat or butter, milk and vanilla essence. Whisk with an electric whisk on medium speed for about 1 minute. Scrape down the sides of the bowl with a spatula to ensure that all the mixture is incorporated.

3. Add the eggs. Whisk for 1 minute on medium speed. Scrape the bowl down again, then whisk on high speed for 1–2 minutes until well mixed. Spoon the batter into the paper-lined tin to fill each cup about two-thirds full.

4. Bake in the centre of the oven for 20–25 minutes until a toothpick inserted into the centre of a cupcake comes out clean.

5. Remove from the oven. Cool for 5 minutes in the tin, then place individual cupcakes on a wire rack to cool completely.

6. When cold, ice with your favourite icing or decorate as you desire.

GRANNY'S CHOCOLATE CHIP COOKIES

To pass the American grandma test, you have to have a recipe for chocolate chip cookies. To call these delicious, wholesome, chewy cookies biscuits would be a travesty. They are easy and quick enough to make with the grandchildren.

Makes about 40

You will need:
125g (4½oz) porridge oats
110g (4oz) unsalted butter, at room temperature
110g (4oz) caster sugar
110g (4oz) light brown sugar
1 large egg
1 tsp vanilla essence
110g (4oz) plain flour, sifted
½ tsp baking powder
½ tsp bicarbonate of soda
¼ tsp salt
75g (3oz) plain chocolate chips
75g (3oz) milk chocolate chips
75g (3oz) white chocolate chips
50g (2oz) chopped pecans

1.   Preheat the oven to 190°C (375°F/Gas Mark 5). Place the oats in a blender or food processor and whizz until fine, about 1 minute.

2.   Whisk the butter, with both sugars in a large bowl using an electric whisk, until smooth. Whisk in the egg and vanilla essence.

3.   In another bowl, combine the processed oats with the flour, baking powder, bicarbonate of soda and salt. Slowly add to the butter mixture, then stir in the chocolate chips and pecans.

4.   On ungreased baking sheets, drop tablespoonfuls of the dough, spacing them well apart.

5.   Bake until golden brown, about 10 minutes. The cookies will still be somewhat soft. Remove from the oven and cool on the baking sheets for 5 minutes, then transfer to wire racks to continue cooling.

6.   Store in an airtight container.

CONDENSED MILK FUDGE

A great gift idea for family and friends – everyone likes fudge!

Makes about 900g (2lb)

You will need:
500g (18oz) plain or milk chocolate chips
400g (14oz) sweetened condensed milk
Pinch of salt
50–110g (2–4oz) chopped walnuts or pecans (optional)
1 tsp vanilla essence

1. In a heavy saucepan, over a low heat, melt the chocolate chips with the condensed milk. Stir in the nuts, if using, and vanilla essence.

2. Spread evenly into a clingfilm or foil-lined 20cm (8in) square pan. Chill in the fridge for about 2 hours or until set.

3. Turn the fudge out of the pan on to a cutting board and cut it into 2.5cm (1in) squares. Then store, covered, in the refrigerator.

RUM BALLS

This is a lovely edible gift for almost any occasion. If you are giving these to children, just omit the liqueur.

Makes about 575g (1¼lb)

You will need:
200g (7oz) digestive biscuits, pulverized into crumbs
110g (4oz) icing sugar
110g (4oz) finely chopped pecans or walnuts
50g (2oz) cocoa powder
3 tbsp golden syrup
1 tsp vanilla, coffee, chocolate, almond or rum essence
4 tbsp brewed coffee, coffee liqueur or dark rum
Icing sugar, cocoa power or chocolate vermicelli,
for coating

1. In a large bowl, mix all the ingredients together well, except the last one. Form into 2.5cm (1in) balls and dip in icing sugar, cocoa powder or chocolate vermicelli.

2. Put into petit fours cases and store in an airtight container. I keep mine in the fridge.

Wrapping presents

PRESENTATION IS KEY

Finding inexpensive ways of wrapping your gifts does not mean sacrificing aesthetics. It's no good buying a wonderful present if you then shove it unceremoniously in a bag, or make a complete botch of wrapping it. Most people don't find wrapping presents neatly a breeze, so here are some handy hints on how to do it:

✻ Make sure you have plenty of space before you begin, and ensure you have enough paper to cover the present – if it's an oddly shaped gift, it's wisest to put it in a box with tissue paper or you will have a nightmare trying to wrap it neatly.

✻ Have some strips of sellotape ready cut so you are not fiddling about with scissors and tape while you're wrapping.

✻ Place your present in the centre of your paper and bring one side of the paper over the gift until it reaches halfway across it. Then pin down the paper using a paperweight.

✻ Lift the other side of the paper so it covers the side that you have anchored. Remove the paperweight but keep the paper in place with one finger until you have taped down the other side of the paper over it.

✿ With one side of the excess wrapping paper facing you, fold one corner in towards the centre. Repeat with the opposite corner, fold up to enclose the present and tape securely. Then turn the parcel around and repeat on the other side.

THE WRAPPING PAPER

How much money do you spend on wrapping paper every year? I was spending a fortune, given the amount of presents I have to wrap, so I started to look for cheaper, more creative ways to wrap my gifts. I found a local source for very inexpensive brown wrapping paper in a huge quantity. It kept me going for probably ten years – I said it was a huge quantity! All you have to do is buy some pretty ribbon, which you can purchase from a sewing supplies shop rather than a gift shop, and you can often purchase gift tags from charity shops in January when they are half price or less.

BOXES

If you can't get your head around wrapping a present, you can use a chocolate box, or something similar. Just cover it with some nice paper so the recipient doesn't guess your trick!

RECYCLING

Don't reach for the bin once you've finished unwrapping gifts at Christmas or on your birthday. So long as you don't rip open your presents with wild abandon, and ensure that as little paper as possible is torn, you can use it to wrap gifts for other people. Just make sure you re-use the paper for someone other than the person who gave you the present in the first place!

RSVPs

When you invite someone to a party, you expect them to respond and let you know whether they will be coming, right? Well, here I am up again on my high horse because, for whatever reason, they often don't.

A friend of mine invited me to a dinner party for which I was making the dessert and said, 'I don't know whether there will be ten or eighteen.' How do you cook for that? For the larger number, I would suggest, but if someone gives you a telephone number or an email address on an invite to respond to, and you do not reply to them, it is presumptuous to expect them to cater for you. That's not only common sense, it's good manners!

Please reply on or before 20th November 2009

*Mr*_____

*Will be attending*_____

*Unable to attend*_____

The golden rule

'Do unto others as you would have them do unto you.'

Basically this means that you should treat other people with the same concern and kindness as you would like them to show towards you. Give your friends, family, neighbours and even strangers your time, help and friendship when they are in need – who knows when you might need the same from them?